You go girls!

The Woman's Guide to Great Travel

You go girls!

The Woman's Guide to Great Travel

SECOND EDITION

VALISE
Publishing

BY **MARCIA LYNN MILLER**

Publisher: Valise Publishing

Paperback ISBN-13 978-0-578-82893-0

1 3 5 7 9 10 8 6 4 2

Praise for *You Go Girls!*

She's put her many years of travel experience into a book filled with advice and insider knowledge. With information on everything from how to stay safe in your hotel room to recipes for a good foot soak to what to know about renting a car (and driving) in a foreign country, this book is packed with the kind of useful information you'll underline, dog-ear, and return to again and again.

— Kathleen McCleary, author of *LEAVING HAVEN* and *A SIMPLE THING*

Marcia Miller is a knowledgeable, experienced traveler and shares her wealth of experiences to prepare women for their journeys around the world or across the state. The keys to an enjoyable trip are presented in this book in an easy-to-read format; no doubt you will be planning your next excursion before you finish the book. You go girl!

— Gerry Frank, author of *WHERE TO FIND IT, BUY IT, EAT IT IN NEW YORK*

YOU GO GIRLS! is a fun and informative read. Marcia's personality shines through as she takes you through the process of planning and executing a trip, highlighting the countless details you will encounter along the way. Sitting down with this book is like having a nice long chat with a BFF who has amassed a wealth of travel knowledge throughout years of experience. Any woman traveler, from the novice to the seasoned, will find many valuable tips and ideas to ensure that her adventures are safe, fun.

— Barbara Skoch Mendenez, Alaska Airlines, veteran flight attendant

If you're such an experienced traveler, why do you still over pack, under dress, tip too much, sleep too little, get the center seat on the plane, and forget your toothbrush or deodorant every single time? Before your next trip, whether you're going for fun or strictly business, on a boat or on a train, for a week or three months, get your hands on a copy of Marcia Miller's YOU GO GIRLS!, and travel like you've never traveled before. Marcia packs every solitary thing you need to know about taking successful trips into a delightful-to-read package, from tips on sleeping in the air to going strong on the ground; from leaving your pet to coping with a country's pet peeves; from choosing a travel bag to bagging your essentials. What's best, it's all written exclusively for women, because, as Marcia says right at the start: "Women travel differently than men."

— Geri Brin, founder,
faboverfifty.com

From dealing with blisters, to confirming visa requirements, exchanging money, and seeing the sites, Marcia Miller gives you everything you need to know for a safe, informed, and fabulous adventure. Whether you're traveling with kids or on your own, for business or pleasure, YOU GO GIRLS! is a must. And guys, you could learn a lot, too.

— Karen Emmerling, owner,
Beach Books, Seaside, Oregon

Table of Contents

Acknowledgments

Thank you TO KATHRYN AND Ned Rawn for nourishing my body with wonderful food, my heart with friendship, and my soul with that magnificent view. Priscilla Wallace, thank you for your clear thinking that kept me on track. Margo Peifer, your gracious and generous gifts of time and talent were pivotal in finishing this project correctly.

Ellen Heltzel, you "got me" and put the words in tune, thank you.

Gerry Frank, Lisa Gardner, Marion Gellatly, Cynthia Haskins, Richard Horswell, Maureen Hovenkotter, Brenda Kinsel, Kathleen McCleary, Honey Perkel, Val Ramsey, and Leslie Sbrocco all authors in their own right kept me motivated to stand among them.

Debbie Cairns, thank you for such a complete and professional approach to your subject.

Red Mountain Spa, your soft place between the rocks forever remains special to me as the place that cradled the birth my book.

You Go Girls! alumnae, thank you for your encouragement. You have taught me so much; without you I am nothing.

Thank you, mom and dad, for giving me wings.

Hunt and Clay, my exotic journeys meant that you grew up with my missing some birthdays and sporting events. Thanks for your understanding of my wanderlust. Now a new generation follows my globetrotting. Grandchildren make staying home a rewarding adventure, and their grasp or the larger world makes my heart soar. Eric, you deserve medal for holding down the home front as husband, dad, and Dude. "Thank you" is an expression too small for my gratitude. I love you for never doubting my pursuit of this project. Thank you for letting me live my dream.

Because Women Travel Differently Than Men...

A BOOK EXCLUSIVELY FOR THEM MAKES PERfect sense. People around the world laugh when I say that about women. Their first snappy retort is that women pack more shoes than men. But this about more than espadrilles, stilettos, clogs, and loafers. It is about the attitudes and attributes women bring with them as they navigate the world. Consider:

- **Women gravitate to relationships that feed social connections.** That's why I started my business, You Go Girls! Travel. It's built on the concept of small escorted group tours to cultivate positive relationships on the road. During my decades in this business, I've encountered so many women who are kind and supportive of one another.

- **Women have different physical challenges than men.**

Just because we have less muscle mass and different body types than men, we don't have to feel vulnerable. Consider that Indira Gandhi was an impactful 5'3", Judge Judy is a 5'1" petite powerhouse, and Dolly Parton at only five feet is an entertainment and business mogul. If instinct and intelligence didn't trump upper-body strength, the human race would be in big trouble!

- **Women know how to be flexible.** At home we read body language and interpret social cues. When traveling, those cues change, and we must adjust. In some places, women violate local norms by traveling alone, so we find an option such as joining a group tour. We may need to change our wardrobe choices or behaviors to fit local expectations. This is not the time or place to prove a point. With proper research, we are capable of making wise choices to keep us safe, without missing any adventures.

What is holding you back? What is the worst that can happen? Your experience and intelligence have brought you this far. **Listen to your heart and, use your brain.** That is exactly how women assess the new situations presented when traveling. If your heart tells you to be afraid, use your brain to guide you. Listen to what your emotions tell you. Use your intelligence to guide your steps. The simple fact that your emotional center is sending you a message needs to cue your brain to listen, assess, and respond in a rational way.

Travel teaches many lessons. It teaches the wisdom of being prepared and the confidence to take control of the surroundings. It gives immeasurable pleasure, wonderful memories, and a wider world view. Have you noticed that woman who is poised and comfortable in her surroundings, in spite being far from home? Here is the knowledge you need to become that woman!

CHAPTER 1

Who Started This?

My FAMILY VALUED TRAVEL. WE PLANNED our own trip to Mexico in 1963, before the Internet, electronic banking, and cell phones. We owned a small travel trailer for domestic road trips. Instead of a suitcase, each of us was assigned a small drawer in the trailer. It was about half the size of a carryon bag. Packing efficiently was not an option. It was mandatory. That was my introduction to packing light.

At 15, I spent the summer studying Spanish in Mexico. During my college years, I spent a semester in Austria. That was where I caught the travel bug. After a succession of unsatisfying post-college jobs, with one notable exception– the one where I met my future husband – I followed my passion and became a travel agent.

After entering the travel industry, I discovered how many women shared my wanderlust but perceived obstacles in their path. They were either single or had partners like my husband, who preferred to stay home. They were curious but did not want to travel alone. I saw an unmet need and an opportunity: What if I could find other women who wanted to travel, could create unique opportunities for them, and I could go along?

In 1999, I founded You Go Girls! Travel to take small groups of women – 20 or fewer – on trips around America and around the world. I have been to over 70 countries. I've seen firsthand how travel offers not only a chance to learn but also to influence the direction of women's lives.

The itineraries I create blend the best of sightseeing with plenty of free time to explore personal interests. With You Go Girls!, women travel in the supportive company of other interesting women but also can indulge in personal interests ranging from bird watching, to speed-walking, or sitting in a street-side cafe.

My job on these trips is best described as "social director" and "crisis manager." The first task is to keep people happy and comfortable. The second set of responsibilities involves the 24/7 handling of any inevitable travel glitches – and with a smile on my face – whether the crisis is a cancelled flight, a health emergency, or a missing passport. With travel, as with life, you can't depend on the weather. Purses get stolen, and people get lost, sick, and hurt. I have handled medical issues from an appendectomy on an Antarctic cruise to an arm fractured in three places in the cloud forest of Costa Rica. I have been mugged in Ecuador – a not-so-pleasant memory – but I may have saved a man's life on a remote jungle hike.

Now when I pack, I am packing for as many as 20 people, answering their questions and guiding their choices. I have learned from each of them. It is fun to share it all with you.

HOME AND BACK AGAIN

I spend four to six months a year on the road. And even when I am "home," I am often not at home. My husband and I split our lives together between a house in Portland, Oregon, and a vineyard near Yakima, in eastern Washington state, where we grow wine grapes that are sold to vintners from the West Coast to Connecticut. Does that make us a little bit country and a little bit rock 'n' roll? In the city I have theater, food, a wine tasting group, and grandchildren. In the country I tend a beehive and a garden while enjoying friends under the starry night sky. When people ask my favorite destination, I'm not being glib when I answer, "Home." It is my touchstone, and my travel schedule reminds me to appreciate it.

But travel remains central. Even when I'm home, I am visiting the closets of my fellow women travelers to advise them on what to pack. I conduct packing demonstrations and give travel advice both in person, in print, and on the air. My ultimate thrill comes when a client asks herself, "What would Marcia do?"

A woman in my morning exercise class asked if I could answer a question after class. She was preparing to leave for Australia the next day and wanted a recommendation for a sleeping medication for her long plane ride ahead.

I could hardly believe it: This woman had less than 24 hours before departure and was seeking medical advice from me. *Yikes, lady, you need a doctor – and not just someone who plays one on TV. Furthermore, you should have begun this process months ago.*

I started down my mental checklist and, not surprisingly, got responses that revealed what I feared: Our conversation was too little, too late to save her from the possible problems she could encounter on her trip. What a shame, when proper preparation would have taken her trip from good to great. But where could she have found out what she needed to know? She confirmed that there is a need for all this information to be compiled into one book.

Over the years, I've learned so much from the wise women who have gone before me as sisters of the road. Building on their wisdom and my own experiences, I began composing a book that could prepare any woman to go anywhere: a weekend getaway, a Caribbean cruise, her first trip to Paris, or a six-month sabbatical. Using these guidelines *does* make a difference. The quality of your travel experiences *will* improve. You *can* make planning, packing, and traveling easy and more relaxing and, in the case of business travel, more productive.

This book is a gentle guide and not a bible. Take what works for you. The space in the margins was created to let you make your personal notes and reminders. Armed with information, you will be that calm and confident worldly woman.

Together, let's move through the standard steps of planning, packing, flying, sightseeing, and even returning home. Invite me to sit on your bed while you pack. We will make everything fit in your luggage and stay under the weight limit allowed for your bag. I'll share the secrets of staying comfortable on the plane even if you're stuck in a middle seat. I'll show you how to dress appropriately for your walk down the Champs-Élysées, or wherever else it is you're going. On the return home, I'll be there to help you unpack your bag and decompress from your trip. We will have fun sharing stories – yours, mine, and those of some of the other women with whom I've traveled.

CHAPTER 2

Ready – Or Not

It HAS BECOME INCREASINGLY EASY TO GET FROM point A to point B in the world. Modern jet travel, high-speed trains, and stabilized ships have removed so many of the barriers to travel. But increasing geo-political challenges have added new worries and threats to travel at home and abroad. It is an act of faith to step out into the world and believe you will be safe or will at least be prepared to take care of your self in any situation.

Each of us must develop our own mindset to allow us to take that step out the door.

If you have ever painted a room or given yourself a manicure, you know the most important step of the process is the preparation. Travel is no different. Every journey begins with that first step. It is the most important. To get started you will need some information, guidebooks, shoes, a purse, and maybe a passport. Then you move on to considering insurance and visiting your doctor. And that is just the beginning.

ENJOYMENT IS IN DIRECT PROPORTION TO PREPARATION

There are no truer words I can offer. I've seen people miss sites they had their hearts set on seeing because they didn't know they needed a reservation. They have passed by important places because they didn't recognize their importance. Others looked foolish because they did not understand local customs.

Once you decide on your destination, the next step is learning about it. **Expose yourself to as much information as you can handle.** Get *into* your destination and let it get *into* you. You chose it; now embrace it with all the energy you can muster. Immersion is an important element in achieving satisfaction, according to happiness expert Elizabeth Dunn of the University of British Columbia. It will enhance the appreciation of your experiences in so many ways.

- **Develop a reading/watching list.** The Internet puts a library at your fingertips, and a simple search quickly produces ideas as does the local library. Longitude Books has wonderful suggestions waiting for you. Ask your neighborhood bookstore for more personal direction. Look for novels as well as nonfiction. Watch movies and TV shows. Find cultural events and exhibits related to your trip. Art exhibitions, dance troupes, and musical acts from all over the world perform in most major cities.

- **Get a taste for your trip by dining in ethnic or regional restaurants.** Knowing the food and its ingredients provides great insight into your destination's agriculture, climate, geography, and culture. For instance, when you know the local bread is cooked in a certain type of oven that burns a special species of wood, you already know more than most visitors. You will recognize kiva ovens in Zuni pueblos and appreciate how far the walk is to find fuel for it.

- **Talk with friends – or friends of friends – with advice to share.** When you put your plans out into the community, you'll find connections, and they will find you. People love to share their stories. Soon you will be the one with tales to tell, and I know you will share.

- **Take a class.** Local community colleges, park bureaus, and continuing education programs will help you build the base with classes that are destination-specific or address the regional politics, religion, cuisine, and language. Take one with a friend or make a new friend in class.

Great travel tip: What you really need to pack is a good attitude and a smile. Take them out and use them often.

- **Learn simple foreign phrases** like please and thank you. You will be amazed at the doors that open.

ANTICIPATION IS MORE THAN A SONG IN A KETCHUP COMMERCIAL

Your trip occupies only a small piece of time. The planning and the memories last much longer than the trip itself, and anticipation may be the sweetest pleasure of travel. At least, according to a study from The Netherlands that was published in the journal *Applied Research in Quality of Life,* it's not just the vacation, but looking forward to it, that determines how much you value the experience. Just as the

7

mouthwatering anticipation of a piece of chocolate cake tomorrow steals our attention, so does the dream of basking on the beach in Bali.

As you dream about that impending vacation, your brain paves the way by creating positive scenarios. You imagine a pleasurable experience – no flight delays, no spilled drinks, no lost luggage. Meanwhile, you get the material benefits of careful advance planning:

Great travel tip:
Be sure you know the payment schedule for your trip. When are deposits and final payments due?

- Your budget is spent creating a great time, not on late booking fees.

- You have greater availability of rooms, flights and activities.

- You pay lower rates.

- You avoid errors by having the time to consider your decisions.

WHO YOU GONNA' CALL?

Your head is spinning with questions. Where am I going? What will I do there? How much will it cost? How much time do I need? When should I go? Travel planning is a huge project to tackle alone.

YOU NEED PROFESSIONAL HELP

"Do It Yourself" (DIY) travel became an option when technology made it easy for airlines to sell directly to passengers via the Internet. That also allowed them to stop paying commission to travel agents. DIY took off and travel agents were grounded.

The stories I could tell, of nice people making horrible travel decisions based on their own research, could curl your hair. They have wasted money purchasing the wrong rail pass, stayed in bad or poorly located hotels, and overpaid for airline tickets, resulting in wasted time, and unnecessary frustrations.

Countless online searches will lead you to a myriad of travel products and services. You can spend hours of screen-time looking and comparing. You think you are saving money, but there is a chance of making mistakes due to your lack of knowledge or experience. You use professional to prepare your taxes, fix your car and cut your hair. Your travel plans deserve the same consideration.

An accomplished travel agent has resources to get better and faster results to save your money. Most agencies are members of buying groups or consortia that negotiate reduced rates with hotel chains, cruise lines, tour operators, and airlines. Those benefit you.

No travel agent can guarantee smooth sailing with a clear sky and the wind at your back. But it is nice to have one in your corner, working on your behalf. Your vacation dollars are valuable. You worked too hard to earn them to put them at risk.

As a result of the 2020 pandemic, many people had travel plans disrupted. They swore to use a travel agent for their next trip. Spending interminable hours trying to reach airlines, getting conflicting answers to questions, not understanding travel jargon, dealing with hotels in different countries, and other frustrations have driven travelers to understand and appreciate the services of travel professionals.

HOW TO FIND A GOOD TRAVEL AGENT

Finding a travel agent is like finding any other professional. You use the same processes that you do when seeking a new dentist or accountant?

Look for certification

A high level of commitment to professionalism and knowledge is required to achieve a certification. The alphabet soup offered by the Travel Institute include CTC (Certified Travel Counselor), Certified Travel Associate (CTA), and Certified Travel Industry Executive (CTIE). Destination and Lifestyle Specialists have mastery of specific destinations and travel styles. Ask a prospective agent if they have completed any of these programs to assure that you are dealing with someone who respects the industry and takes their work seriously.

Seek recommendations

Friends are a good source of referrals. They often share your interests and are familiar with your expectations. People you know can lead you with an agent whose work style, personality, and experience meet your needs.

Interview each other

Be ready with a list of questions. A good travel agent may have more questions for you than you will for them. Be open and honest. They need to your travel style, budget, interests, hobbies, level of physical health, limitations, and more. The more they know about you, the better they are able to serve you. They are sort of like therapists – there is nothing you can say that will shock them.

Question them about their certifications and experience. Other subjects should include fees and working hours (many agents work from home). Ask what buying groups or consortia they are a part of. These are key in being able to offer you the best pricing, upgrades and value-added items.

Most travel agents are happy to work WITH you. They welcome your input and ideas. You can still be as involved as you want to be in the planning. Listen to their expertise and remember they have planned thousands of trips. They have the ability to make your trip easier and save you money.

GUIDEBOOKS

A one-size-fits-all guidebook does not exist. Some cover hotels and restaurants well. Others focus on sightseeing. Still others give block-by-block walking tours of historic, architectural, and cultural sites. Most do one thing well and contain marginal information on other subjects.

To find the best one for you, start with three free resources, the bookstore, the library, and the Internet. All can show you a free preview of guidebooks you might wish to purchase. Amazon, for example, shows sample pages. Michelin, Frommer's, Fodor's, Rick Steves, Moon, and Lonely Planet all publish reliable guides. The DK series is superb for sightseeing information.

Once you buy the book, make it work for you. As hard as it is to tear out pages, to do so makes perfect sense. Why carry the chapter that deals with hotel recommendations when you already have your reservations? If you need only the walking tour map of Florence, take only that piece. The other option is to make photocopies. When you're done with them, recycle: Many hotels have a lobby or library where departing guests can leave books. What goes around comes around.

Every day there are more and more guides available to download. Rick Steves now offers audio guides for many cities. Load them onto your electronic device, put in your ear-buds, and off you go – not particularly sociable but effective. There are also travel apps for smart phones, from maps to museum guides. **Download those guides before you go.** Be careful about using your expensive phone on the street. Stay aware of your surroundings when wearing headphones or earbuds. You could miss warning cues in traffic and crossing streets, and you are an easy target for theft

MAKING IT OFFICIAL

Armed with your itinerary and guidebooks, what else could you possibly need? For international travel, there is one more must-have item.

Where is your passport? When does it expire? To get a new passport use this link: travel.state.gov/content/passports/english/passports/apply.html. The forms and instructions are all there. You must apply *in person* but will have everything in order by following the instructions. To *renew* your old passport, use this link: travel.state.gov/content/passports/english/passports/renew.html. Most renewals can be done online.

Do you need any visas for the countries on your itinerary? It is YOUR responsibility to know. Check with your travel agent, your air carrier, and the consular webpage for guidelines. It is up to you to do the research. There is no flexibility on this. Visa requirements change and depend on your country of citizenship, reason for travel, and length of stay. You will need to confirm the current requirements for any country you are visiting or passing through. You will be denied entry without proper documentation. That is an expensive mistake.

Once you know the requirements, you can acquire the necessary visas yourself or **choose to pay a visa service** to facilitate the paperwork. One such company is VisaCentral, which can be found at visacentral.com.

Is it safe to visit <u>(fill in the blank)</u>? For U.S. travelers, the State Department lists warnings and other advisories at travel.state.gov.

Purchase travel insurance before your departure. If you travel abroad, your medical insurance probably does not cover you there. Insurance is discussed in more depth in Chapter 8.

A visit to your doctor or travel clinic is one of the most critical items on your preparation list. Complete coverage of this subject is in Chapter 14.

CHAPTER 3

What to Pack

What YOU TAKE TO WEAR IS ONE ISSUE. The other things you need are quite another. The most important items in your suitcase aren't necessarily your clothes. In this chapter, let's take a look at the other potential "essentials."

PICKING AND PACKING A TOTE BAG

You are not a "bag lady." Look like a pro.

The advantage to not checking luggage is to know your bag is going to arrive with you. The drawback is that if you pack too much, it is cumbersome and can slow you down. In most cases, international carriers allow one bag in addition to a carryon sized suitcase. They do not allow a carryon suitcase, a small carryon tote, a handbag, computer bag, and backpack.

Consolidating your things into two reasonable pieces, is one of those things that can take your travel from good to great. You will look like a traveling pro – unlike the young woman I watched board a plane with a hatbox, a backpack, a shopping bag, and a purse! Your best accessory on a plane, train, car, or bus is a tote. When I say tote, I mean a secure, small carryon bag different from a carryon sized suitcase.

Pick your price point, whether from Target or Saks Fifth Avenue. The most important requirement is that your tote meets any size or weight requirements for the transportation you choose.

Should you have one with wheels? Carrying a heavy bag on your shoulder while maneuvering a larger one through airports and down sidewalks is tiring and makes you more vulnerable to theft – a dangerous combination. If the large bag has a handle with two vertical posts, you can use a tote with a sleeve on the back that allows it to slide over the handle of the larger bag. A single-post handle lets the top bag tilt, twist, or fall without further support.

Consider having these items in your tote no matter what mode of transportation you are using.

- Medications
- Contact numbers for those meeting you, hotel and airlines
- Headphones, for listening to your music or downloads Noise-canceling headphones are best for long, loud flights
- Computer: Never pack your valuable computer in a checked bag.
- Cell phone: It is at risk if placed in a checked bag.
- Mechanical pencil: You need it for your crossword puzzles. No need for a sharpener.
- Pen: Immigration/customs forms must be completed in blue or black ink, and pressure-sensitive copies require a ballpoint. Take two so you can lend one to your seatmate.
- Book or electronic reader
- Water
- Evian Facial Spray or a spray bottle of water for freshening

- Earplugs, especially if you don't have a noise-canceling headset. They will turn off an overly chatty seatmate on the plane and shut out street sounds or amorous neighbors at your hotel.
- Inflatable pillow
- Toiletries: Pack only things you cannot live without. I carry my makeup with me because it would be difficult to replace, and it fits in a very small zippered bag.
- Toothbrush/toothpaste: A fresh mouth is a great pick-me-up. Do not drink water from the airplane restroom. It is usually not potable.
- Eye drops, because eyes dry out in an airplane.
- Nose spray. Check with your doctor. Keeping mucus membranes moist could aid in fighting sinus issues.
- Pashmina: Some type of shawl will keep you warm and looking polished.
- Two bandanas: Keep reading to learn their many uses.
- Hand sanitizer
- Slippers or flip-flops: Feet swell on airplanes, and the bathroom floors are gross. Even when traveling by car or train, give your piggies a break.
- Nightgown, in case you and your checked bag do not meet at your destination.
- Change of underwear, in anticipation of that lost bag situation.
- Keys – if you are going home. Ah, yes, I know this story: What if you arrive home and your bag doesn't, but the keys to your car and house are in the missing bag?
- Bathing suit/cover-up: If you are going to a resort and might have some waiting time before you can check in, or on a cruise or tour where there could be a long delay before your

bag is delivered to you. Proceed straight to the pool for an umbrella drink. Hurray for planning ahead!

THESE BOOTS ARE MADE FOR...

You are probably headed for a lot of walking. Regardless of your destination, you need comfortable shoes, you want them to be attractive, and they must fit in your luggage. Sadly, that usually means limiting yourself to two or three pairs. Whether you are a business or leisure traveler, space and weight are your major concerns. This calls for "shoe control."

Choose your shoes carefully and break them in before you take them on the road. And comfortable shoes don't have to be ugly. You will be treated with greater respect when your footwear matches the image you want to convey, this is especially true if you are traveling in Europe or fashion-conscious cities. Unless you're going on a run, nothing screams tacky like white sneakers. Ecco, Clarks, Easy Spirit, Mephisto, Naturalizer, Cole Haan, and many other shoe manufacturers offer attractive, wearable options in a range of prices.

Water retention and heat cause feet to swell, turning what was formerly just a little tight spot into torture. Look for the adjustability of laces, Velcro®, buckles, and elastic. Leather gives you a flexibility that fabric does not. Thick platform soles and stilettos are deathtraps when walking on uneven surfaces or cobblestones. I have seen my share of twisted ankles along the way. A low heel or flat will provide more stability and boots are a winter winner.

Will you need shoes that can stand up to rain or snow? Do you expect weather that will necessitate waterproofing? Consider any speciality shoes for activities such as horseback riding, après ski, hiking, boating, etc.

Bandages or moleskin will protect a sore spot. Use it as soon as you feel a hot spot developing to avoid a painful blister later. Carry them with you during the day. They won't help if they are back in the hotel room. A variety of padded insoles and heel grips are useful for those areas that tend to cause you problems.

When circumstances allow, you can take a wardrobe of shoes. On a recent car trip I have to admit to having taken a laundry basket full. And if you're headed to a tropical resort with light clothing and you have room for extra shoes, go for it. But when air travel is involved, shoes often become the "make or break" item. Don't let your shoes hog what little space and weight allowance you've got.

In the early days of You Go Girls!, I learned a valuable lesson while escorting a 10-day trip through Austria and Germany. I'd brought two pairs of shoes. But a string of 90-degree days and a hotel with no air conditioning quickly revealed that my new pair of black patent leather sandals shouldn't have come along. They were

Great travel tip: Always pack a pair of flip-flops. They hardly weigh a thing and can take you around the plane and the hotel room as well as the pool and the shower. You can exclude them from your total shoe count. Best of all, they are small and lightweight. Keep a pair permanently in your travel bag, and make sure they are the kind that can get wet. If you find a pretty pair with some embellishment or a slight heel, they could provide a dressy shoe option too. If it works, attach a silk flower or other decoration to dress them up and expand their use.

too new, too tight, and uncomfortable. For the balance of the trip, I was forced to wear my one remaining pair. I realized then that, in a pinch, one well-chosen pair could do the job.

In the Chapter 4, you will see how proper wardrobe planning eliminates the need for many shoes.

CHOOSING A HANDBAG

You say handbag, I say purse. Call it what you will, this choice is one of the most important ones you will make before you leave town. Begin by identifying your needs.

Ask yourself:

1. What items must you carry with you for the day?
2. Do you need to carry special items, such as a laptop, supplies for baby, medications, samples, files, or a change of shoes?
3. Where are you going? Are you visiting sophisticated cities or national parks?
4. What are you doing? Will you be in business meetings, sitting on the beach, or attending a film festival?
5. How are you traveling? Are you getting on and off various modes of transportation, in a car or on a boat? Is a small plane or a bus tour limiting your bag size? Will you be able to leave things on the bus while you tour?
6. What are your special needs? Do you need to have hands free for hiking or climbing stairs?

As with clothing, you can layer purses. Yes, layer! The tote you carry on the plane can hold your day bag, which holds your wallet, coin purse, or business card holder that may double as a small clutch for evening. I call it nesting, and it frees up space in your suitcase.

In order for you to be safe, comfortable and fashionable, consider the following four handbag features:

- **Security.** This is the top priority. Your bag should zip up tightly with no openings in order to keep it safe from purse-picking hands. That means no drawstring or snap closure. When traveling in a high-risk area, use a safety pin to "lock" the zipper closed. Just run the pin through the zipper pull and through a part of the purse to help deter theft. **Do not ever carry anything of value in your purse. And if someone wants to take your bag – let him or her have it.** No accessory is worth risking your life or an injury. Carry your bag cross-body to make life hard for thieves. In some countries, women hug their backpack against the front of their body; watch the locals and follow suit.

- **Ease of Carrying.** The right-sized handbag is one that's large enough to carry what you need and light enough to not injure your back or shoulder. Being able to carry it on your back or cross-body distributes the weight more comfortably. The weight, shape, length of strap, and material contribute to its comfort. A cross-body leather messenger bag is too hot for Thailand. A wicker clutch will be silly at the Grand Canyon. A large backpack will not fit under your seat if you are attending a conference.

- **Ease of Use.** Your bag should keep things well organized. A huge bag is not helpful if everything in it falls into a pile in the bottom, no matter how fashion-forward it is. Use zippered pouches to organize the contents. Label them so you know what is in each one or use clear ones. Having to tame an oversized or heavy bag does not convey the impression you want. You need to be in charge and not appear vulnerable. If you want your hands free for getting off and on boats or climbing stairs, look for a bag that can be carried as a backpack or worn cross-body.

- **Fashion Appropriateness.** Let your destination determine the appropriateness of your choice. A straw bag is perfect in Hawaii, a microfiber messenger bag is super in Seattle, a casual backpack is wonderful in Yellowstone, and a sophisticated leather bag is a necessity for fashion-conscious Madrid.

PACKING

Lack of planning and last-minute packing lead to over-packing. Allow plenty of time, and keep pen and paper at your bedside for those moments in the night when you wake up thinking of one more thing to add to your packing list. I use one with a light to make quick notes without waking my husband.

The list I give to my clients has evolved over the years. DO NOT TAKE EVERYTHING ON THIS LIST. It is a generic guide for all types of trips. The concepts are the same whether you are traveling by air, boat, car, or rail, for pleasure or busines. Most of the items are explained somewhere else in this book.

Marcia's You Go Girls! Packing List

- ☐ Toiletries
- ☐ Flashlight
- ☐ Earplugs and eye shades
- ☐ Moisturizing eye drops
- ☐ Lip balm
- ☐ Bandana or two
- ☐ Inflatable travel pillow
- ☐ Tote or light backpack
- ☐ Shopping bag
- ☐ Light jacket for evening and/or airplane
- ☐ Granola bars or snacks
- ☐ Camera
- ☐ Binoculars
- ☐ Electrical converter/adapters
- ☐ Chargers for electronics
- ☐ Portable power source
- ☐ Replacement batteries
- ☐ Extension cord
- ☐ Maps
- ☐ Journal or notebook
- ☐ Pen
- ☐ Mechanical pencil
- ☐ Highlighter pen
- ☐ Post-It notes
- ☐ Fat rubber band
- ☐ Waterless hand sanitizer such as Purell

- ☐ Toilet paper or personal wipes
- ☐ Tissues
- ☐ Antibacterial liquid soap such as Dial liquid
- ☐ Washcloth in Ziploc bag
- ☐ Sunscreen
- ☐ Insect repellent
- ☐ Simple first aid items
- ☐ Pictures of family and postcards of hometown
- ☐ Face mask
- ☐ Small gifts
- ☐ COMFORTABLE SHOES and a back-up pair
- ☐ Laundry supplies – see Chapter 4
- ☐ Small Ziploc bags
- ☐ Large black plastic garbage bag
- ☐ Duct tape, twine, and mailing tube
- ☐ Swiss Army knife
- ☐ Corkscrew
- ☐ Soft-sided cooler
- ☐ Safety pins and sewing kit
- ☐ Talcum powder – maybe medicated
- ☐ Umbrella/parasol
- ☐ Hat and gloves
- ☐ Sunglasses
- ☐ Extra eyeglasses or contact lenses
- ☐ Glasses repair tools
- ☐ Magnifier

Here are some miscellaneous tips to go along with the list.

Most European hotels do not **supply washcloths**. Take an old one you can throw away. Take two if you are on an extended trip. They tend to mildew if you carry them from hotel to hotel when wet. The microfiber ones dry quickly. Find them in Dollar Stores.

Duct tape is the answer. I don't know the question, but duct tape is pretty much always the answer. Hopefully you don't need the whole roll. The end of an old roll or some tape wrapped around a pencil gives you what you need for that MacGyver moment. I have used it to construct a shipping box, keep the curtain closed, pad a handle, patch a torn luggage corner, and for countless other things.

Sewing kit –If there is not one in your room, you will have to request one, but most hotels have them available. If you are going on a budget or to remote places, take your own. A needle and some clear nylon thread will work for the repairs of any color.

Tape measure and swatches – Not very many places in the world use our Imperial system of measurement. Taking your own measuring device will help you judge sizes and find things to fit your table, bed, windows, and more. Take fabric or paint swatches to easily match your clothing or décor at home.

Razors – If you travel with a companion, take just one razor handle. Each of you can take your own blade to pop on it. No need to each take one.

Ziploc bags and garbage bags – At home, I am sparing in my use of plastic bags. When I travel, they are a guilty luxury. They are a wonderful way to carry electronic cords, picnic supplies, and left-overs. A large garbage bag doubles as a poncho, tablecloth, or tarp to protect things from the rain. Keep one folded in your suitcase for an emergency.

A **plastic tablecloth** from the Dollar Store is handy for picnics on your bed or on the grass.

Safety pins – Add a small, medium, and large safety pin to your packing list. They can secure a hem, repair your glasses, hold a bra strap, or keep your blouse button from exposing the girls.

Rubber band – Obvious uses for a rubber band are to keep a poster rolled up or gather hair into a ponytail. Have you ever used one to expand your waistband a little- maybe when you were pregnant? Loop it through the buttonhole with a slipknot and pull it across to hook it to the button. Do you know how to use it to open a water bottle? It can be hard to get ahold of and open the screw-off cap of a stubborn water bottle. Wrap the rubber band around the top a couple times, grab a hold and unscrew. Keep one in your purse.

Extra eyeglasses – You wear glasses because you need them to see. If you lose or break them, you will be able to replace them in most parts of the world if you have the prescription, so take it with you. Contact lens wearers, you should take **back-up glasses**, no matter how old or ugly. An eye infection, wind, or allergies could make you glad to have them. Carry an **extra pair of contact lenses also.**

That little screw in the eyeglass hinge is often a problem for me. **Carry a tiny screwdriver with extra screws.** They come as a set. Keep it in your toiletry bag or purse at all times. Mine came with a small magnifying glass to make it easier to perform the task. In a pinch, replace the screw with a small safety pin or even a paper clip looped through it. You can even use the wire from a plastic bread bag closure by stripping away the paper in a real emergency.

Being able to read maps is critical when you're trying to find your way in a new place. But sometimes the print is so small it is truly impossible to read. A **magnifier** will help, and even a small plastic one can take the strain out of trying to read tiny map printing. International travelers are accustomed to people of many cultures wearing face masks. With the 2020 pandemic, the practice came to our shores. It is always a good idea, even absent the pandemic, to have a good quality medical grade N95 face mask to protect yourself and others. It may also enhance your comfort in places where there is heavy air pollution.

LIGHTS OUT

Stash a **small flashlight** under your pillow. Where is the bathroom and where is the light switch? I hate to hit that fan switch instead of the light in the middle of the night. Girlfriends, countless times that little flashlight has gotten me to the loo and back without a stir from the roommate or a gouge out of my shin. There are also **flashlight apps for your phone.**

No flashlight? Leave the bathroom light on with the door closed. The sliver of light emanating from under the door is just what it takes to remind you where you are and to create a safe passage. Some people pack a nightlight. That works, but it has only a singular use. The flashlight performs a multitude of tasks.

Torches, as they are called in England, are now very small and effective. Use one to read the menu or theater program. It serves to light the way on a dark path or sidewalk. How about using it to check under the bed before you check out of a hotel room?

THE HUMBLE COWGIRL

For many years, I have traveled with my trusted $1 cotton bandana. I taught my clients to do the same. In fact, I usually provide themed ones for my group tours. Look for the 100% cotton ones. They are softer and more absorbent than the cotton/poly blends. If you doubt how useful one bandana can be, look at these ideas. This is the best $1 you will ever spend on a travel item. Take two of them.

100 Ways to Use a Bandana

- ✓ Ice bag
- ✓ Ankle wrap
- ✓ Cheer with your team colors
- ✓ Dry hands – one of my personal favorites
- ✓ Wipe off a dirty or wet chair
- ✓ Protect shoulders from sun – you will need two for broad shoulders
- ✓ Placemat
- ✓ Napkin
- ✓ Mark a trail
- ✓ Tourniquet – heaven forbid
- ✓ Wrap a package
- ✓ Sweatband
- ✓ Arm sling
- ✓ Brush sand off feet
- ✓ Clean car window
- ✓ Clean computer screen
- ✓ Clean camera lens
- ✓ Clean eyeglasses
- ✓ Protect head from sun
- ✓ Wrap a water bottle or glass to catch condensation
- ✓ Wrap a wine bottle to catch drips
- ✓ Wrap a snack
- ✓ Wrap leftovers
- ✓ Wipe fingerprints off the gun – uh-oh, you have a problem

- ✓ Hat band – change up your look
- ✓ Blindfold for a game
- ✓ Dust mask
- ✓ Germ mask
- ✓ Car window shade
- ✓ Wave to rescuers
- ✓ Eye mask
- ✓ Mark your Christmas tree
- ✓ Cooling – wet or wet and freeze it to wrap around the neck
- ✓ A fashionable neck accessory
- ✓ Temporarily repair a hose leak
- ✓ Mop a spill
- ✓ Wear as a pocket square
- ✓ Clean out your wine tasting glass – another personal favorite
- ✓ Remove makeup
- ✓ Clean a wound
- ✓ Door stop – fold it to make a wedge
- ✓ Magic trick accessory
- ✓ Give as a gift
- ✓ Pick produce into
- ✓ Pad something fragile
- ✓ Wrap shoes or handbag to protect from scuffing in luggage
- ✓ Washcloth
- ✓ Dishcloth

- ✓ Tie a ponytail
- ✓ Use as a rag curler
- ✓ Strainer
- ✓ Protect a table from a vase
- ✓ Drink coaster
- ✓ Nose tissue
- ✓ Dab a spot or stain
- ✓ Play peekaboo with a baby
- ✓ Baby bib
- ✓ Apron
- ✓ Entertain a child
- ✓ Play flag football
- ✓ Play capture the flag
- ✓ Hot pad
- ✓ Save a seat
- ✓ Cover a rock or stump to avoid dirt or pitch
- ✓ ID your beverage glass
- ✓ Conceal wine bottle for a blind tasting
- ✓ Hide something
- ✓ Wipe soda can top
- ✓ Secure something rolled – like a poster
- ✓ Carry an injured small animal
- ✓ Roll jewelry in
- ✓ Hold on to pull a child's tooth
- ✓ Ear warmer
- ✓ Lobster bib
- ✓ Wrap as a bracelet

- ✓ Pad a tool handle to prevent a blister
- ✓ Apply pressure to a wound
- ✓ Tie up a plant
- ✓ Shine shoes
- ✓ Blot lipstick
- ✓ Dog collar
- ✓ Puppy toy
- ✓ Bookmark
- ✓ Mark your campsite
- ✓ Tie on car antenna to help locate your car
- ✓ Pad luggage handle
- ✓ Mark the way to a party
- ✓ Pad your camera neck strap – mine cuts into my neck
- ✓ Clean bird droppings off your coat – stuff happens!
- ✓ Relay baton
- ✓ Hobo costume
- ✓ Tie a bouquet
- ✓ ID your luggage
- ✓ Form a comfortable handle for a box tied with twine
- ✓ Change a warm light bulb
- ✓ Cover an airplane pillow
- ✓ Surrender
- ✓ Belt
- ✓ Check wind direction
- ✓ Coffee coozie

CHAPTER 4

Clothes

It TAKES CAREFUL CONSIDERATION TO CURATE A collection that is comfortable, adaptable, appropriate, and easy-care. Your goal should be to find the most options with the fewest number of pieces. That translates to all of those pieces being real work-horses. An efficient travel wardrobe is an important key to taking your travel from good to great. You can create the impression you want to give the world while functioning at your highest level of energy. Imagine a photo of yourself strolling the ruins of Pompeii with the right shoes, outfit, and purse. Now pack for it.

TRAVELER KNOW THYSELF & THY TRIP

Your packing and traveling will go much easier if you first stop to consider who you are and what you are doing. Before you put a thing into your bag, get a clear view of what you need.

1. What activities will you be doing? Sitting in the lodge knitting or hitting the slopes?

2. Are you attending special events? Weddings, trade shows, funerals, or football games?

3. With whom are you traveling? Are there children or your new beau?

4. Where will you be eating? Restaurants, business lunches or picnics?

5. Where are you going? Is there a specific need to dress modestly?

6. What will the weather be like? Check the seasonal averages.

Great travel tip: Sites such as journeywoman.com offer great information for women travelers. Not fitting into the norms of a culture sets you apart and increases the chance that someone will take advantage of you. It says you are a stranger. In some places, that is a downright dangerous position for a woman.

We are guests wherever we go, across the U.S. or around the world. Out of respect for our hosts, we *do* need to care about how we are perceived. Out of respect for ourselves, we must look and behave as though we deserve to be treated with respect.

THE EMPRESS'S NEW CLOTHES

Travel is tough on clothes. Spots happen. Every time I deplane from a long flight, I am covered with spots on my lap or down my front. Travel clothing is worn for long hours and is stressed by getting on and off buses, elephants, bikes, boats, and everything else. It is sad to ruin a brand-new piece the first time you wear it on the road. Save it to show off to your friends at home. **Travel with older items** or things you do not care about. I still want you to look polished and presentable but not to put your special pieces at risk.

Take **a pair of leggings, yoga pants, or stretch pants.** They can be worn to breakfast in the hotel or down the street to grab a take-out pizza. They are comfortable to wear for lounging in your room. Sleep in them if you want. They are super for sleeping on the train or plane. If the bathroom is down the hall you will be making the trek modestly.

Look for **jackets, pants, and skirts with pockets.** Obviously you will not carry anything of value there, but an extra place to carry things is a great benefit. Unfortunately it is difficult to find women's jackets with inside pockets, but I love them. You can always have a tailor add one. They are a convenience for carrying things you want easy access to, such as your boarding pass, pen, map, or cell phone.

Color Your World

During a packing consultation, my client had darling clothes spread all over the room. There were cute outfits everywhere - a great gauzy, flowing black and white blouse with black shorts, a flattering pair of tailored brown pants with a pretty peach sweater set, and a cute embellished, blue cardigan with a print skirt that would satisfy many needs. Each and every individual piece was a winner.

All the outfits would travel well. They were washable and packing-friendly (they could be folded or rolled and survive the trip relatively wrinkle-free). BUT - there was one big BUT. They did not play well together. They were not even in even in the same color or style family. Brown and blue, tailored and hippy chic had my head spinning!

Packing a usable travel wardrobe is easier when you follow these simple guidelines:

1. **Choose a neutral color or two.**
2. **Add one or two accent colors.**
3. **Pack separates.**
4. **Stay within a style family.**

Choose a neutral color or two. Wardrobe planners and image consultants have written volumes about using a neutral color family because it works. Black and gray, navy and white, and brown and khaki are good examples. I even have a client who chooses turquoise and lime. Use just one color if that works best for you or that is what you have in your closet. Very likely it will be your hair color. Most importantly, do not stray. If you choose black and gray and at the last minute toss in your favorite navy pants, you are creating a problem. Suddenly you need shoes, accessories, a coat, and tops to coordinate with that single item. You MUST stick with the system.

Within the United States, you have a palette of bright color options. In some cultures, bright colors or bold prints may mark you as strange or different. Also take care in choosing white, ivory, or very light pastels. They are difficult to keep clean.

Add one or two accent colors. Your accent colors are a chance to express yourself and the way you are going to add interest. Don't go wild. Stay with just a couple or you will compound your problems. Are you going with turquoise, red, tangerine, or a sunny yellow? It is your choice.

Pack separates. The flexibility of separates makes them invaluable. By changing one piece you create a whole new look. You have seen fashion magazines show you how to do it. Nobody you see tomorrow will notice the same black pants from today if you have changed your top.

Stay within one style family. Mixing things from differing styles is a recipe for disaster, even if they are in the same color family. You cannot pair a classic trench coat with romantic ruffled skirts and peasant blouses. See what I mean? One style family will help refine your number of shoe styles, jewelry styles, and outerwear choices. And that is a good thing.

Find your color family AND style family and move with purpose in that direction.

Begin by scouring your closet for what you have, fill in with accessories. Add comfortable shoes and you are ready to go. Please don't sing me the blues that you will get tired of those clothes by the end of your two-week trip. I have heard it all before. By mixing them up and accessorizing, you will survive and will be ready to appreciate your wardrobe at home when you return to it.

This system is not boring. You will add interest to your neutral basics with accent colors, prints, and accessories to finish your look. It is easy to get ready in the morning with a good wardrobe of basics and a choice of other pieces that all coordinate with them. You could almost get dressed in the dark. And with those early flights, sometimes you do exactly that.

I warn against making a plan in advance to wear a certain outfit on a certain day. Weather, mood, and activities are subject to changes. If all your items coordinate you know your choice in the morning will be an easy one once you assess the conditions.

PLANNING THE PACKING

Begin with a list, a plan, and enough time to think things through. The natural result of packing well leads you to pack light. Proper planning leads to good choices. Tossing things into a suitcase the night before you leave inevitably results in poor choices and over-packing. A list is the best way to remember everything and to take only what you really need.

Using the Form

For years I have been using this tool to streamline my packing. It is just a simple form you can make yourself on a sheet of paper. **Mix and match all outfits on paper before committing them to the suitcase.**

1. List bottoms on the left side of a page – pants and skirts.

2. List tops down the right side of the page – tees, blouses, and sweaters.

3. Draw a line from each top to the bottom with which it could be worn.

    Each bottom and each top must have AT LEAST TWO matches. It is usually easy to wear a bottom piece more than once without laundering. It is not as easy to wear a top twice. Be sure you can hand launder or safely send all pieces to the laundry. Remember, you must usually be in your hotel for 2 nights to allow time for the laundry to be returned. Choose tops that require minimal care. You are not on a trip to spend time ironing.

4. Underneath make a list of your shoe pairings. Be sure you have a pair for each combination of top and bottom.

Flats could be one option with a black skirt and sweater. A short heel goes with the same black skirt and a stretchy lace blouse for evening.

10 DAY FALL TRIP TO CHICAGO

BOTTOMS

Brown pants

Brown skirt

Tan pants

Herringbone pants*

TOPS

Cream long sleeve knit*

Brown turtleneck

Paisley blouse

Tan sweater

OUTERWEAR

Tan puffy vest*

Brown trench coat*

SHOES

Brown short boot*

Brown patent loafers

SPECIAL EVENTS – items

Lunch downtown – Brown skirt

Jazz club night – Tan pants

Joy's birthday – mom's scarf

ACCCESSORIES

Coral and bone beads

Brown/tan necklace

Crinkle coral scarf*

Gold chain necklace

Gold bangles

Pearl necklace

Mom's scarf

Warm hat - brown

Gloves – brown

Shawl w/metallic

thread

Tan pashmina

* Wear on plane

5. On the bottom, note any special pieces you need, such as a bathing suit, cover-up, evening wear, Kentucky Derby hat, strapless bra, hiking boots, wetsuit, etc. This is also the place to list the accessories to stretch your wardrobe and make it interesting, expressive, and fun.

The Shoe Solution

Choosing shoes in your neutral or accent color solves your problem. They will match everything. Assess your needs and opt for your best styles. Is it boots, loafers, water-shoes, or sandals for this trip? Your feet will thank you if you take two pairs to alternate.

ACCESSORIES MIX IT UP

Packing challenges us to plan ahead for living in a confined space with finite resources. This can seem frightening but fear not. Variety is achieved with accessories that change your looks while taking minimum space and weight.

Accessorizing is more than knotting a frumpy old triangle silk scarf around your neck or clipping on some plate-size earrings. **Learn to use accessories as part of preparing for your trip.** Assess your basic travel wardrobe pieces and then invest some thought into what accessories will take them up a notch.

Scarves are an accessorizing basic. They can be tied in hundreds of different ways, sporty or sophisticated. They are functional in adding a layer of warmth or blocking the cold. They bring attention to your face and color to your ensemble. Tie one onto your handbag or in your hair. Use one to cover your legs when needed.

Belts add interest without taking much space in your luggage. Roll them up and stick them in a shoe, or wrap them around the inside of your suitcase, flat against the sides. I don't favor belts when I am going to wear my coat all day. The belt is hidden and adds uncomfortable constriction. But if a belt can be seen and is flattering to your body type, pack it.

Legwear kicks it up in cooler climates. Think how different a brown pencil skirt and brown sweater can look with bright orange tights, leopard print hose, striped leggings, or glittery mesh stockings. They do not take a lot of space and are not heavy. Take a duplicate pair in case of a run.

A wardrobe consultant is a valuable resource if you lack confidence in making wardrobe choices. The salesperson at a local department or specialty store can help. Or consult a fashionable friend.

Bling

Jewelry does not take a lot of space and is a perfect way to jazz up your neutral travel wardrobe. Necklaces, earrings, pins, and bracelets brighten any look. Carry them with you and don't put them in a checked bag. Do not take any jewelry you would regret losing. I'll tell you later about having a $35 necklace stripped from my neck. Just because it is not valuable does not mean it is not a temptation to a thief.

Use costume jewelry. If a classic look is your thing, look for attractive pieces that are not valuable precious metals. For a more creative style, find artistic pieces that express your personality at local art fairs. Places like Chico's and your local department stores offer interesting items too. Jackets, sweaters, or shawls with a metallic thread or sparkle add interest in place of jewelry.

To avoid tangling small necklaces and bracelets, run each through a straw and close the clasp. Cut the straw to size and put the jewelry in a container such as a glasses case, pencil case,

Great travel tip:
Pack your jewelry in your carryon bag to get it safely to your destination.

or jewelry roll. Larger pieces may require a box. Put rubber bands around the container in both directions to keep the lid on.

Put all your jewelry together in one place so you are not searching all over to find that one small thing. There are all sorts of jewelry cases, boxes, and rolls available. **Keep both earrings of a pair together** to make them easy to find. Options for packing them include- Ziploc bags, silk pouches, 35 mm plastic film canisters, or pill bottles. For pierced ears, be sure you have the right backs for each pair. The universal plastic ones are easy. Take the stabilizing discs if you need them. You can use a pencil eraser to replace a missing back if needed.

Take enough accessories to jazz up your wardrobe and express your personality.

THE MISCELLANY OF CLOTHING

What other items might you want to consider when packing? What makes something a good choice?

Fabulous Fabrics

Knits, wrinkle-resistant fabrics, and pieces without details such as ruffles are easy travel pieces. Knits really do travel well. Technology has improved woven fabrics, too. Those new stain-resistant and anti-wrinkle properties help make an item travel-friendly. The addition of stretch qualities to so many garments is proving to be a lifesaver for travelers. The stretch makes wearing them easy and comfortable. You can get right on that elephant without risk of splitting your pants.

Girlie Stuff – The 34B

Here is some bra news you can use. Most packing lists suggest a certain number of bras. Do you know it is not good for a bra to be worn two days in a row? It needs to rest for a day to regain its stretch memory. Pack two, bearing in mind what tops you will be wearing. If you need a variety of specialty bras, I recommend a good convertible one to serve more than one purpose. You do not need a halter bra and a T-back and a strapless if you have a good convertible. If you like a clean bra each day, do a little laundry in the hotel sink.

Pashmina Forever

Pashmina is really a specific type of cashmere fiber, but generically it has come to mean a shawl. How funny that my two favorite travel accessories are both merely rectangles of fabric: the cotton bandana and the shawl. In colors from coral to black and in weights from voile to almost felt-like, my shawls serve many purposes. Fold yours flat. Stick it into a large Ziploc and carry it in your handbag or tote. It will stay clean and fresh. You will be warm and ready for anything, anywhere.

- Freezing in the airport waiting area? Wrap it around your legs.
- Cold on the plane? Substitute it for the absent airline blankets.
- Drafty in the theater? Rescued by shawl.
- Icy cruise ship dining room? Save the meal with the shawl.
- Entering a church wearing a sleeveless top? It gets you in the door.
- Wind blowing your hairdo? Protect it with the shawl.
- Legs feeling a bit exposed when you sit? Got you covered.

- Need to spruce up that neutral basic outfit for evening? Accessorize yourself.
- Grand entrance at the pool? Splashing with your shawl wrapped as a skirt or dress.

Practice to become comfortable with different ways to wrap or tie it. Google "how to wrap a pashmina" or "how to tie a shawl." There are hundreds of ideas from boleros to head-wraps.

Great travel tip: Want your shoulders covered and need your hands free from the distraction of a loose shawl, try this. It works beautifully with a large scarf and can be used with your lightweight shawl, too. Tie the two corners on the skinny end together with a tiny knot. Then tie the opposite end corners in the same way. Use just a little tiny knot on the very ends. Slip your arms through the ends and you have created sort of a cocoon that will stay on without your hands having to intervene.

Fashion Alert – 5.5 Deadly Sins

Much of the travel I do is in European and American cities. My cautions come primarily from the fashion horrors I have witnessed in those settings. All of these items have an appropriate use. Here are the ones I consider the 5.5 Deadly Sins, along with some alternatives for avoiding them.

1. Shoes that don't fit the scene

Historically, no self-respecting Parisian woman would be seen in her workout shoes except in the gym. However, athletic shoes have now made an entrance as a fashion item. I still caution that there is a difference between fashionable white sneakers and your old tennis shoes. Be sure your look fits the location.. Their weight and use of suitcase space alone would be enough to deter me from sneakers unless I am going someplace where I really need them, and they are appropriate.

There are many stylish comfortable shoes available. For an example, black patent oxfords could wear like a tennis shoe but convey a completely different impression. They work great in the rain and look fine with a pair of pants or skirt and tights. A good pair of boots adds style to any outfit. A flat pair of boots in a classic riding style has gone all over Europe with me for years.

The same holds true for sandals. The clunky outdoor sandals you wear hiking or boating, are not acceptable in the city. Metallic gold sandals might be adorable in the urban setting but not hiking in the Black Forest. Be mindful.

2. Backpacks

There is a time and a place for a backpack, and there are many backpack styles. Hiking in the Tyrol a casual nylon backpack serves perfectly. A Louis Vuitton pack could be acceptable in Paris. A leather Healthy Back Bag converted to its backpack form works for shopping in London. Many better hotels, restaurants, and shops pull up the welcome mat for pack-clad guests. Not only do they downgrade the ambiance of the joint, when carried on the back, packs knock over displays and break fragile items. Shopkeepers also see them as a vehicle for shoplifters.

With a bag in its pack incarnation, it will behoove you to

remove it and carry it as a handbag when entering a shop or stopping at the Ritz for a glass of champagne.

In a New York City hotel lobby, I saw a young woman asked to leave because she was wearing a backpack. In many museums, you are allowed a handbag but not a pack. The problem in museums is in the wearer bumping against the art. A large pack also takes space almost equivalent to another person. **Where people are jostling for position to view artworks or artifacts, it is considerate to remove it from your back.**

Backpacks can save your shoulders and your back, as opposed to carrying a heavy handbag on your shoulder or in your hand. Find an attractive bag that looks like a nice handbag and converts to a backpack. I have one I love so much I often forget to change it out when I get home. It is bronze metallic leather with straps that pull to morph it for wearing on the back. In the purse form, it is an attractive bag and shows no sign of being a backpack. See what you can find to make a proper impression while still being practical.

3. Casual Coats

In cooler weather, a coat is often the only visible item of your carefully chosen outfit. That makes it important to wear something that reflects the overall style of the location. A casual waterproof anorak is great for hiking, attending an outdoor concert, or boating. It will not fly in the city. A trench coat and umbrella or a raincoat and hat are polished and appropriate looks there.

4. Zip-Off or Convertible Pants

Pants with legs that zip off to become capris or shorts are a great idea. I wish I had invented them. That does not make them acceptable everywhere. They are very casual and made out of fabrics suitable for hiking. If you are rafting the Salmon River, hiking the Inca Trail, or bicycling along the Danube, you should get some. They are not for city wear. If the temperature swings enough to require you to change your clothes at mid-day, use layering to your advantage. A pair of leggings under your skirt in the morning can come off in the warmer afternoon. Or wear warm socks that can be removed later. Create some options for yourself.

5. Shorts

Please check whether shorts are appropriate for your destination. In European cities you will not see local women wearing them. Yes, you might see them on a boating vacation in the countryside but not in the city.

.5 Jeans

Blue jeans are my .5 struggle. I have had to change my tune over the years. For years I ranted that they are too casual for most big cities and Europe. Now, women of all ages, in all places have made them the uniform of the world, even in fashion-forward cites such as Paris, Madrid, and New York. I am not going down without a fight on this subject. It is not the silhouette I am opposed to but rather the worn-out mom jeans that look like you just came in from gathering flowers in your garden. Those with careless accessorizing are not OK. I confess to taking a pair of good black jeans on some recent trips to Europe. They have served well in casual places, doing casual things in the countryside, and on some very cold days with long underwear under them. Be aware that jeans are heavy to pack, hot to wear, difficult to wash, and take a long time to dry in a hotel room. You might want to wear them on the plane and not pack them due to their weight.

A basic color pant in twill or microfiber is a good and versatile substitute. In cooler climates, gabardine or wool flannel works well. For warmer climates, choose a linen or chino.

If you make the choice to wear stylish blue jeans in an urban area, pair them with nice accessories. A darker wash or black creates a dressier impression. And by all means, if you are at a dude ranch or in a rural setting, they are fine.

Cool Clothes

Fit and fabric are the keys to staying cool. **The fit should be nonbinding, loose, and flowing.** A loose dress allows for air to move, making it cool and comfortable. Clothing that touches your skin holds in heat. This translates into discomfort and sweat stains on your clothes.

Clothing fabrics need to be breathable as well as have wicking properties. Traditionally, we think natural fibers such as cotton and linen are cool, but technology has created new materials with special cooling characteristics, among them **Supplex and CoolMax.**

Great travel tip: A black or nude camisole is a great layering piece for hot or cold. Wear it alone or use it for layering. Get the kind with the shelf bra. Then to round out your bustline and cover the nipples, pop in foam bra cups. Find them in the lingerie department. Voile, no bra straps.

THE HIERARCHY OF RAIN PROTECTION

Proper handling of warm or cold weather contributes to your comfort level. Dealing with precipitation is another critical aspect of that. I live in a wet place. We have a whole vocabulary to describe what falls out of the sky. We have words like rain, showers, mist, drizzle, and more. But do you know the words for the fabrics to protect you from them? The definitions of waterproof, water repellent, and water resistant are the difference between dry and drenched. Here they are:

BEST: "Waterproof" is the highest level of protection. Water cannot penetrate these fabrics. Truly waterproof garments are constructed with sealed seams to prevent moisture from passing through the needle punctures on the sewn seams. Waterproof items are generally more expensive than water repellent or water resistant ones.

BETTER: Water repellent fabrics have the quality of keeping water out to some degree but not completely. They may have a finish on them that comes off with wear or cleaning.

GOOD: Water resistant means that moisture cannot easily penetrate these fabrics. DWR (Durable Water Repellent) is sometimes the treatment used to achieve the resistant property. You may see it on the hangtag of an item. These pieces also can lose resistance after time or washing.

Mama Bear Was Too Hot

We know that cold temperatures do not give you colds, germs do. But being uncomfortable from heat or cold is a stress to your body. Here are some tricks to keeping comfortable when the temperatures fall.

Layer it up. Long underwear does not have to be bulky. For a light layer, try silk. There are catalogs and stores that use a grading system to gauge the warming qualities of long underwear. There are also new, fast-drying fabrics with wicking characteristics. Sporting goods stores are a good source, as are online stores such as Wintersilks. As an alternative to long underwear, layering a T-shirt or turtleneck under a sweater might be enough. A pair of leggings or tights can add warmth under your pants.

A **Thermacare heat wrap** on your core provides pleasant heat all day. It was a cold and damp day at Stonehenge when I hit upon this idea. My back ached so I slapped on the wrap and enjoyed both relief and the side effect of being warm. They stay warm for several hours. If yours is still putting out heat at bedtime, stick it at the foot of your hotel bed to take off the chill.

Use accessories to your advantage. Hats seal in the heat that would be lost from your head. A warm scarf around your neck seals in the heat of your torso. You can also pull it up over your mouth for extreme cold. Warm socks help your feet, as do insulated insoles inserted into your shoes. Gloves are great. A light pair and a crushable hat are kept packed in my wintertime travel bag.

Make a cup of hot soup or tea. You have to love those countries where tea is the drink of choice and hotel rooms have electric teakettles. Heat up some water to combine with an envelope of soup mix, hot chocolate, or whatever. No kettle or coffee maker? Take one of those little immersion heater coils. They are inexpensive and easy. Just don't leave one unattended. They are hot.

TAKING CARE OF CLOTHES

If you pack light, you are probably going to need to do some wash. Sending things out for laundering is a risky proposition. You lose control over their treatment. Hotel laundries do not understand cold wash, gentle cycle, and line dry. Heaven knows how hard the rock is on which they will pound your panties. I have had them returned crispy from water that must have been boiling. They were literally melted, giving new meaning to "hot pants."

Laundomat in a Bag

If you have concerns about the cleanliness of the hotel sink, wipe it with an antibacterial cleaner before using it, or make your own "washing machine" in a plastic bag. This is also a great idea where water is not plentiful. Put the clothes in the bag, fill with water and soap, swish, empty the water, fill again with fresh water to rinse, repeat the rinse and you are good to go. Thank you, Wendy, for the sharing your great system.

A trip to the local laundromat is sure to provide you with some stories to tell. It seems I always meet someone interesting there. Take change and a good book. On a long trip it is sometimes just best to include some time to do all the laundry at once. You can do multiple loads at the same time. It feels good to have all your clothing clean.

Dropping off your laundry at the neighborhood cleaners can be

---

CREATE YOUR OWN LAUNDRY CENTER

A soap product such as Bio Suds is easy on the environment. Tide makes travel-size packets, too. That's an item to find at **minimus.biz.**

Tide to Go and Shout Wipes provide a fast fix for emergency stain treatment. They tuck easily into a purse or pocket.

Toss in **a universal sink stopper**, one of those flat ones. Hotel sinks often do not have an effective stopper.

A hanger and some clips or clothespins make drying a snap. Many hotels supply those hateful hangers that do not come off the closet rod. Having just one hanger, wire, plastic, or inflatable can make drying so much easier.

Taking **your own clothes line** is a good idea. Some hotels have them and others don't. The twisted elastic ones don't even need clothespins.

an option in the city. It is less expensive than the hotel service. But you must be in one place long enough to enjoy this luxury.

For those times when an item is not quite dry when you need it, **use the hairdryer to speed up the drying process.** Just be careful about using too much heat on synthetics.

Another handy item is a **hook that goes over the door**. It can hold your purse, your wet coat or the outfit you plan to wear the next day.

Never drape clothes over a lamp. Why would anyone think to tell you that? I think you can guess. I nearly burned down a Paris hotel by drying my tights on the wall sconce. The melted nylon dripped into the sconce and burst into flames. Fortunately, I was there to extinguish them… but it could have been otherwise.

Try to avoid clothing that requires dry cleaning. If you must pack some, keep the items fresh longer by wearing a camisole or washable tee shirt underneath to protect them from perspiration, if styling and climate permit. Depending on your needs and the fabric, you have a couple of options for those "dry clean only" pieces. Either send them out for dry cleaning or look into freshening with a product such as Febreze or Dryel.

Be very careful with travel irons. I hate to iron at home, so why would I do it on a trip? If you decide to travel with an iron, you don't want to be the person who leaves a melted iron imprint on the bedspread or carpet. But be advised that most cruise ships do not allow irons aboard. The risk of accidental fire is too great. Ask if your ship has a self-serve laundry.

An alternative to an iron is a portable steamer. It will not burn down the hotel or char the bedspread. Or try hanging your item in the steamy bathroom. In a pinch I've been known to

Great travel tip: The easiest way to escape the laundry detail is to choose travel-friendly colors, fabrics, and styling.

lightly sprinkle or mist a tee shirt and then blow it with a hair-dryer while tugging it a little to pull out wrinkles. **Downy Wrinkle Releaser** will perk up a tired top. Simply spray, tug the piece and small wrinkles disappear, leaving you with a fresh-smelling garment.

CHAPTER 5

Packing It In

Once YOU KNOW WHAT'S GOING INTO YOUR bag, you wonder how on earth you're going to get all of it to fit. Are you going to need a steamer trunk and a team of Sherpas? Fear not – we have solutions.

PACKING RIGHT MEANS PACKING LIGHT

What is the big deal about packing light, and why is it so important? The answer is two-pronged. The first is that you have to handle that luggage. The second is that the airlines are going to charge you plenty extra for checking those big, heavy bags.

We travel to experience other places, to experience their uniqueness, and to enjoy the journey. When we are slaves to our possessions, we are not free to experience, explore, or enjoy. Being in a constant state of worry over losing a bag or misplacing a favorite item compromises our ability to "be" in a place. We become emotional captives of our possessions.

Multiple pieces of heavy luggage are difficult to handle and to monitor. Lighten your load and free yourself.

Once you are on the train to Timbuktu and can lift your bag onto the tiny overhead rack, you will kiss the ground I probably have walked on. As soon as you lug your bag up the stairs in a charming Italian villa, you'll sing my praises. Being hot, exhausted, and unable to pull your bag onto the shuttle at Heathrow does not paint a picture of confidence. Being at the mercy of a strong man to lift your bag won't make you look or feel capable, either.

Be in control of yourself and your belongings. Always move and act like you know what you are doing. You are a capable woman who can navigate the world on your own terms. See yourself that way. Act the part.

Here is the deal. There is no sugar coating it and it is probably not what you want to hear. **THE PROBLEM IS NOT YOUR PACKING TECHNIQUE BUT TAKING TOO MUCH.** I have never heard a traveler return to say that they wish they had taken more, quite the contrary.

Lighten Your Load

The high cost of checking bags makes it seem logical to cram as much as possible into the fewest number of bags. Okay, I'm a master of that. But watch out, there is also a mandated maximum weight limit on bags. The simple reality is that there are only two ways to lighten the load: **Get a lighter bag, or reduce the weight of what's inside.**

Use technology to your advantage. Luggage manufacturers are using new, stronger, and lighter materials for bags. When purchasing luggage, **find out what it weighs.** This is often displayed right on the label. A lighter bag may mean the difference between paying for an overweight bag or taking an extra pair of shoes!

Don't take so much stuff. That is the ugly truth to packing light. You can roll it, fold it, compress it or use whatever other system you can devise. It will not help or only will help minimally at best. The simple truth is that you must reduce the load. Sorry about that!

Personal Supplies

Pack amounts in proportion to the length of your trip. Just because the Transportation Security Administration (TSA) allows 3-ounce bottles doesn't mean you need 3 ounces. You may need much less than you think.

- A 3-ounce bottle contains 6 tablespoons. You probably use about 1/2 tablespoon of shampoo per hair washing. That translates to twelve uses. Do you wash your hair daily? If so, then you have almost two weeks of shampoo in a 3-ounce bottle. Calculate how much you need for your next trip. At the very end, add a bit of water to stretch it the last couple of days if you fear you are running low. If math isn't your strong suit, put 3 ounces of shampoo in a bottle and use it at home to see how long it lasts. Now you know!

Great travel tip: To transfer liquids from the big bottle to a small bottle use the system from easytravelerinc.com. Using simple physics they make it so easy. Use the code GOGIRLS at checkout for a discount.

- A 0.75-ounce travel size toothpaste tube yields over 9 inches of product. If you use 1/4 inch per brushing, twice a day, your supply will last 18 days.

- Carry the smallest versions of your regular personal products. There are three ways to shrink them: Choose samples or travel-size, or transfer your own products into smaller bottles. Sample sizes work well, but **this is not a time to test a new product.** Waking up with hives in Helsinki could spoil your trip! Ask for samples of tried-and-true products that work for you at your favorite cosmetics counter.

Go to **minimus.biz** for absolutely anything in a travel size. It is the only place I've found small containers of Mitchum deodorant. This site covers everything from head to toe, hairspray to foot powder, and shipping is fast. I've met the owner and toured the facility and am confident they will take good care of you.

Collect small plastic bottles to fill with your favorite products. Try to find square ones. They fit together better in your one-quart plastic bag; and use less space than round ones. Look for ones that are leak-proof.

To help prevent leakage in your checked bag, squeeze the air out of plastic bottles and cap them. Then **put any liquid-filled containers in a Ziploc bag**.

The world has become a very connected place. Pharmacies in foreign countries are some of my favorite places to visit. It is not a big deal if you forget your toothbrush, and so what if you run out of shampoo? Venture into the local market to buy some. If the weather turns cold and you need a warmer sweater, shop for one. Every time I leave home I say to myself, "What can I *not* leave without?" Usually the answer is just my passport. Really!

Packin' the Hat

I love hats. They are an absolute necessity in some situations and a fun accessory in others. But how do you pack one? It depends on the hat and the situation, but here are some guidelines:

Wear It. This is often the best option, unless you need to pack a fancy hat for a wedding or special event. You would look pretty silly sporting your huge Kentucky Derby chapeau through the Chicago airport, and pity the person seated next to you on the plane.

Get a Hatbox. Oh, how I long for the drama of arriving with a gorgeous round box containing some dreamy concoction. However, in today's world, that means an extra piece of luggage with the associated fees and security issues. But a girl's gotta do what a girl's gotta do. Go ahead if it is that special. Your hatbox can become your carry-on bag if it fits within the airline's requirements for size, and you can be sure you'll get the attention of the other passengers.

Pack It. Gently stuff the inside of the hat with socks, lingerie, or whatever fills it up. Set it, upside down, into the bag on top of a layer or two of clothing. The next step is to gently nest more items around it, sandwiching it on top. Depending on the delicacy and value of the hat, wrap it in tissue or plastic to protect it from soiling. Another option, if its size and shape allow, is to place it in a box and pack the box in your bag for more protection.

Most cold weather hats are soft and pack easily. Summer hats present more challenges. Look for packable ones that will roll or fold.

Hat Etiquette

While on the subject of hats, let's divert just a minute to consider proper hat etiquette. Until as recently as 1983, women were required to cover their heads when entering a Catholic church. As a visitor in someone else's house of worship, how do you know the proper protocol? Take your cues from those around you, but here are some guidelines:

The easy rule is **if it is an outdoor hat worn for protection, it**

should come off. In general, if your hat is a part of your outfit, such as a pillbox hat matching a Chanel suit, you leave it on inside the church. Visualize the Duchess of Cambridge in this situation. If you are wearing a hat for warmth or protection, it comes off, as does your winter rain hat or knit hat. A visor or sunhat comes off. A nice straw hat or fur hat matching your coat sits on the cusp. It may or may not come off. And when wearing a baseball style hat, it follows the same rules as when a man wears it. It comes off without question.

For the playing of our national anthem, a woman may keep her hat on unless it is a baseball hat or other unisex style, in which case it comes off. At a rodeo, a woman wearing a cowboy hat has the option to take it off or leave it on. Watch what the rodeo queen does. You pretty much cannot make a mistake by taking off a hat for anyone's national anthem. When abroad, follow the natives.

Admittedly, it can be confusing. Just remember, ladies, **it is hardly ever an error to remove your hat.**

SPEAKING OF BAGS

Carrying luggage is exhausting and can potentially cause injury. I propose that if you cannot carry your bag around the block by yourself and up three flights of stairs, it is too heavy. How are you going to lift it off and onto the train car within a short connection time? How can you get it into the overhead compartment of an airplane? How are you going to carry it up those narrow stairs in your European hotel with no elevator?

According to the U.S. Consumer Products Safety Commission, more than 72,000 people were treated in 2014 for injuries caused by handling luggage.

American Academy of Orthopedic Surgeons (AAOS) Recommendations

These smart doctors urge you to use proper judgment when packing, lifting, and carrying luggage. The Academy offers the following tips for lifting and carrying luggage:

- Look for a sturdy, light, high-quality and transportable pieces when shopping for luggage. Choose luggage with wheels and a handle. Avoid purchasing luggage that is too heavy or bulky when empty.

- Use smart packing techniques and pack lightly. When possible, place items in a few smaller bags instead of one large luggage piece.

- To lift luggage, stand alongside it and bend at the knees. Try to limit bending at the waist. Lift the luggage with your leg muscles. Grasp the handle and straighten up. Once you lift the luggage, hold it close to your body.

- Do not twist when lifting and carrying luggage. Point your toes in the direction you are headed and turn your entire body in that direction.

- Do not rush when lifting or carrying a suitcase. If it is too cumbersome, get help.

- Do not carry bulky luggage for long periods of time. When possible, use the airline's baggage claim service when traveling with heavier items.

- Carry pieces in both of your hands rather than one hand off to the side. This can decrease stress to the spine. Less weight on any one arm can also reduce the risk of developing "suitcase elbow," a chronic condition similar to "tennis elbow."

- When placing luggage in an overhead compartment, first lift it onto the top of the seat. Place your hands on the left and right sides of the suitcase and lift it up. If your luggage has wheels, make sure the wheel-side is set in the compartment first. Once wheels are inside, put one hand atop the luggage and push it to the back of the compartment. To remove the luggage, reverse this process.

- When using a backpack, make sure it has two padded and adjustable shoulder straps to equally balance the weight. Choose a backpack with several compartments to secure various-sized items, packing the heavier things low and toward the center. Slinging a backpack over one shoulder does not allow weight to be distributed evenly. This can cause muscle strain.

- When using a duffel or shoulder bag, do not carry it on one shoulder for any length of time. Be sure to switch sides often.

- Do not drag rolling luggage when climbing stairs. Carry it, instead.

Great travel tip: Use caution wheeling your bag onto escalators or moving sidewalks. Keep a good eye on what is happening ahead of you and do not board too close to others. When the family in front of you has trouble disembarking with all their kids and bags, you could be caught in a vulnerable position. Look for an elevator.

Leave Room to Come Home

You are going to shop, aren't you? How are you going to get those goodies home in your bag? What if they don't fit? Do you need the item next week? How easy is it to carry this package for the balance of your trip? Is the item valuable or breakable? Here are some options to weigh.

1. Take an extra bag with you. If you do, you will pay the cost to take it and get it home.

2. Buy a bag at your destination and you will only pay for the trip in one direction, but you will spend valuable time shopping for a cheap bag.

3. Mail packages home – an iffy and expensive proposition. Some countries have horrible theft issues with their mail. Shipping times can be lengthy.

4. **Take an extra foldable soft-sided bag**. If you need the auxiliary bag, pop it out and load it up. You can fill it with dirty laundry or use your laundry to pad the purchases. At least, you will pay the charge for an extra bag only one way and you save time and money shopping for a single use bag.

I like the Baggallini bags for this purpose. Two flight attendants designed them, and they are light-weight and compact. Look for them at most travel stores or on-line.

Take care in packing your *special* mementos to take home. If you want them to get home safely, carry them with you. Evaluate if you want to risk putting them in a checked bag. You could be required by customs officers to present them with their receipts.

Great travel tip: Be honest on your customs declaration on your return to the U.S. They are usually fairly forgiving for truth-tellers. Not so much for liars.

YOUR PACKING STYLE

Packing is a challenge for most of us. The same system does not work in the same way for everyone. If you are on the super-organized end of the spectrum, then consider something like the Eagle Creek Pack-It system. It uses templates to keep things uniformly folded and then packs them into uniformly shaped cubes.

Packing cubes are the current rage. They do help organize. One downside is that they work best when also used to compress items. If you do not pack it really full, you miss out on the compression benefits.

More relaxed packers might simply roll up items on the theory that helps prevent wrinkling and it is easy to see what you have. I am not so sure it prevents wrinkles, but it may help prevent creasing.

Ziploc's Space Bag products allow you to fold or roll items and then compress them to save room in your suitcase. No vacuum is required. They are light, reusable, easy, inexpensive, and are flexible for a variety of items. They are especially good for keeping dirty or damp items separate from the clean and dry.

Good folding and packing help eliminate ironing. The best method is to follow the lines or seams of the garment. Fold

LOSE 5 POUNDS AND SAVE!

Compare the weight of these common items. Where can you save a few pounds and avoid $100 in overweight luggage fees? Small changes make a big difference.

Electronic reader (15 oz.) versus three best-selling novels (1 lb. each) = SAVE 2 pounds

Leather boots (1.5 lb.) versus a pair of shoes (1/2 lb.) = SAVE 1 pound (Wear the boots on the plane!)

Bathrobe (1 lb.) versus using your coat as a robe = SAVE 1 pound

Shampoo & conditioner, full-size (2 lb.), versus 3 oz. sample size = SAVE 1.5+ pounds

Hard-sided 28-inch suitcase (13 lb.) versus lightweight 28-inch soft-sided suitcase (9 lb.) = SAVE 4 pounds

Lightweight 28-inch soft-sided suitcase (9 lb.) versus lightweight 22-inch soft-sided suitcase (6.5 lb.) = SAVE 2.5 pounds

iPad Mini (.68 lb.) versus MacBook (5 lb.) = SAVE 4.32 pounds where it will least likely be noticed. For an item with buttons down the front, fold it in half along the line of buttons. If it has princess seams, **fold it along those seams**. Use tissue or a plastic bag from the cleaners to soften the folds of a particularly fragile item, if you must take it. Consider a hanging bag if it is especially important.

To help eliminate horizontal creases in pants, fold your tops as uniformly as possible and stack them. Lay out your pants and skirts flat and folded lengthwise. Set the stack of folded tops on the middle of the pants and roll the pants around the tops.

Stuff every vacant space with smaller items. Belts, scarves, gloves, and socks can be stuffed into the toe of shoes.

Put heavy items in what will be the bottom of your bag when it is upright. This keeps it from becoming top-heavy, off-balance, and prone to tipping over.

Use the **outside pockets of your bag for things you need to access** along the way.

Wear your heaviest shoes on the plane, keeping that weight and bulk out of your bag.

Great travel tip: Umbrellas are an iffy proposition. They can keep you dry in a shower, but they have their drawbacks. They are worthless in wind and dangerous on crowded sidewalks, where they are likely to poke someone. They are often left behind, they drip, and you need to have a free hand to hold them.

CHAPTER 6

Getting out the Door

Leaving HOME MEANS TAKING ALL possible precautions to make sure the house, and its contents, will be intact when you return. I have had my furnace malfunction and dangerously overheated the house; another time, the pipes froze and then thawed, leaving four inches of water on the floor. No one wants to come home to a Christmas night disaster like I did.

SECURING THE HOUSE

There is no substitute for having a trusted friend or neighbor who can check on your place. Pay someone to do this, if necessary. Ideally, have this person enter your home to check for anything that might need attention inside.

Interior Checklist

- [ ] Check refrigerators/freezers to confirm they are maintaining proper temperatures.
- [ ] Check kitchen, laundry room, and bathrooms for leaks.
- [ ] Check thermostat. The heating/cooling system can probably

be taken down to 50 degrees in the winter and up to 85 in the summer to save money while no one is there.

☐ Are the plants healthy?

Exterior Checklist

☐ Check for mail and newspapers.

☐ Check perimeter for security breaches or break-ins.

☐ Check yard, porch, patio, and decks for papers, circulars, deliveries, etc.

• **If you have a security system,** be sure your house sitter is clear about the password and how to operate it.

• **Stopping the newspaper and mail** service are no-brainers. Hold your mail with the U.S. Postal Service by going on-line to make your request or by using their Form 8076. Newspapers can be called or notified on-line to suspend your delivery. Some, like mine, will issue a credit or transfer the credit to various charities.

• Even the best-laid plans to handle the mail and papers are not foolproof. Newspaper carriers may deliver your paper in the middle of your vacation – this happens to me frequently – and even if you stop your mail, there are always UPS, FedEx, DHL, and door hangers from the pizza delivery man that may show up while you're gone. Someone should be **watching out for unexpected deliveries** or unsolicited circulars that advertise you're out of town.

• Did you cancel your Blue Apron or other meal delivery services too?

- As silly as it may seem to say, **be sure all doors and windows are locked** when you leave.

- **Be careful about revealing your travel plans on social media sites.** You could be announcing your departure to the world, including burglars.

- Do you need to **arrange for your grass to be mowed and weeds controlled** while you are gone? An ill-kempt yard is another signal to criminals that you are away.

- If you have **outside water features,** are they protected from unexpected cold? What about the danger of the fountain reservoir drying up and burning out the pump?

- **Do not leave the washer, dryer, or dishwasher running** when you leave. Hoses break, leaks happen, appliances malfunction, and fires start.

- **Turn off the water to your washer.** It is easy to reach behind the washer to shut off the water supply. Just turn those two handles to the off position.

- **Make a note to remind yourself to reactivate them** when you return. It is frustrating to arrive home jet-lagged and exhausted, go to put the dirty travel clothes in the washer and feel that panic when it doesn't work. Been there, done that!

- **Set heating and air conditioning to accommodate your pets and plants.** Extreme temperatures can become dangerous for any living things inside. Opening cupboard doors under sinks will help circulate warmer air around pipes located in cold exterior walls.

- **Use a timer on your lights** to simulate someone being home. My neighbors leave on the porch light and the microwave light on in the kitchen – a dead give-away that they are gone. Get some battery-operated fake candles with a timer. Put one in the window. No one expects a lighted candle on the sill if someone is away. The fake flicker makes it appear you are home.

- **Leave a radio on** so that it sounds like there is someone inside.

- **Clean out the refrigerator, bread drawer and fruit basket.** Time to toss the leftovers and doggie bags. Rotten bananas and moldy English muffins do not make for a pleasant welcome home.

- **Take out all garbage and empty trashcans.** The aroma of old garbage is disgusting. Clear out all inside trash. Arrange to have outside garbage cans taken to the curb and returned to their normal storage place.

- **Be sure to run the dishwasher** and not leave dirty dishes in it. Just don't leave it running.

- How about your telephones? Do you still have a land line? If so, you might want to **forward your calls to your cell phone.** The ability to receive transcribed voice messages by email avoids international roaming charges that may incur by forwarding them.

- And my personal favorite – **Is the coffee pot unplugged?** How about the curling iron or hot curlers? How many times have I doubled back to check those?

Pets

Pets are a big responsibility. If you decide to keep your pets at home while you are away, you need a checklist for them too.

- **Leave your complete contact information** for the pet sitter.

- **Leave detailed instructions** for the care of your animal, including contact information for your veterinarian.

- **Let your vet know the level of care and expenses you will authorize in your absence**. The vet will have a form you can complete. Communicate your decisions to the caregiver.

- Be sure you have left an **adequate supply of food** for the duration of your trip.

- **Have a back-up plan.** What if your return is delayed and your pet sitter can't stay? What if the pet sitter does not show up? I have a client who lost a valued pet bird because of a sitter's neglect.

- **Get your pet an email address.** Seriously? Maybe not. But friends who care for our dog set up an account for her and send us messages on her behalf while we are gone. We get a kick out of it, and so do they.

CHAPTER 7

Planes, Trains, and Automobiles

Whoever SAID THAT THE JOY OF life is in the journey obviously didn't travel much. Getting there often presents some of the greatest challenges and least pleasant experiences of your trip. The best defense is to take charge of what you can and let go of everything else. Remember the root of the word "travel" is travail – a painful or laborious struggle.

FREQUENT FLYERS

Each airline has a different plan to reward loyal travelers. Buyers beware: To reap the benefits of carrier loyalty, you must play by the rules. The object of this game is to accrue as many points as possible. You win when you exchange points for upgrades, free tickets, and other perks.

Enroll in a plan. It's easy to do online, at the airport, or over the phone, and you will benefit by joining several different plans. You won't accrue points as quickly this way, but you will be building toward the bonus of a free ticket or upgrade.

Once you are enrolled, how are you going to accrue points? There are several ways.

- Fly on that airline.
- Fly on a partner carrier.
- Use the carrier's credit card.
- Use hotels, car rentals, and other services or products that partner with that airline.

Some carriers allow you to purchase points to fill the gap when you are short of miles for your prize. Generally, you cannot transfer points between different accounts, but you can sometimes "gift" points for a fee. And if someone dies, you may be able to "inherit" points.

Keeping your travel goals in mind, decide which airlines and services you are most likely to use. Most carriers belong to systems such as One World Alliance or Star Alliance. As airlines go through mergers and acquisitions, you must pay careful attention to who is part of which alliance in order to maximize your benefits, as they shift often.

Many plans offer an associated credit card, which pay you some amount of points per dollar charged on the card (usually a point per dollar), with bonus points for certain promotions. Additional benefits might include a sign-up bonus, an annual bonus when you reach a certain level, buy-one-get-one tickets, early check-in, and free baggage checking. **Check the terms and fees to see if an airline credit card is a realistic way for you to boost the points in your account.**

Once you stack up an adequate number of

Great travel tip: When a loved one dies, call the airlines to see if you are able to use the deceased's miles. It is a shame to let them go to waste. There is not a universal policy for this but in many cases it is possible.

points, you will be entitled to a free or reduced-rate ticket and/or upgrade. However, don't get your heart set on being able to use them. It can be difficult to redeem points. You must be very flexible. Sometimes the space you want is available far in advance of travel, and sometimes it is not. It might become available closer to your date of departure. It's a tricky game, and I'm not sure there is a reliable way to master it.

When you do find a seat using your points, **research the actual ticket price you would be paying if you were purchasing the ticket**. You probably do not want to use 50,000 points for a domestic ticket worth $250 if that same level of points could get you a free ticket to Europe. Obviously, if you have earned 500,000 points, your decision may be different than the person with only 50,000.

To accrue points, give your member number when you purchase your ticket. If you forget to do that when you purchase, but remember before you travel, the fix is easy. Call the carrier to add it to your record, have your travel agent add it or edit the reservation you made online. After travel, it's more cumbersome: Each carrier has its own process for recapturing the points, all requiring that it be done in a timely manner.

Confirm again at check-in that your number is entered and recorded correctly. Usually it's printed on your boarding pass.

Monitor your account to be sure you received proper credit after a trip. Segments flown on the specific carrier are credited quickly, but those on partner carriers can take longer. Retain your ticket and boarding pass stubs until you are sure you have received the credit for them.

If you are missing credit, check the carrier's website or call immediately for their protocol on handling adjustments.

This covers the tip of a very big iceberg that is still worth chiseling down to your size. You'll be glad you did when you settle into that free, first-class seat to Shanghai.

CHECKING LUGGAGE

Where your luggage goes is, to some extent, out of your control. But there are some ways to improve the odds of it arriving with you. These precautions will help prevent your luggage from going astray.

- **Attach identification tags** to your bags. **Use your cell phone number as the contact.** Your home phone is not helpful to airline personnel if you are not there.

- **Include your itinerary and ID *INSIDE* the bag.** ID routinely disappears off bags.

- **Check in with time to spare before departure.** The cutoff time varies in different airports and is longer for international flights. Your carrier can tell you what time applies to your itinerary. Being late not only increases the risk of losing your bag but also the chance of losing your seat. Be early but not too early; they also will not accept your bag *before* a certain time.

- **Confirm the routing tags placed on your bags are for the proper destination and routing.** Sometimes bags only get as far as your first connecting city or the wrong one. Many airport codes are similar. For example, Kansas City is MCI and Orlando is MCO, just one key apart on the keyboard. SJC, SJD, SJO and SJU are airports in four different countries.

- Bags look alike. **Set yours apart** by attaching a colorful ribbon or strap or by stenciling your initial on the outside. Consider choosing an unusual color for your next bag to help it stand out in a sea of black bags. Double check to **be sure you are taking YOUR bag** at baggage claim and hope others are doing the same.

- **Take a digital photo of your bag.** It will help identify it for a Lost Bag Report. Your cell phone camera works perfectly for this. Photograph the contents as a record of what you packed. If things go missing, you have something to help inventory any potential loss.

There Is No Such Thing as Free Luggage – I Mean Lunch!

It is costly to check multiple or heavy pieces of luggage. Airlines will gladly separate you from your hard-earned money in exchange for checking your bags. They collect an added bonus when a bag is over the allowable weight limit. They do this to make money and we play (pay) right into their hands. The U.S. Department of the Treasury reports U.S. airlines made over $3.5 billion on luggage fees in 2014. And these fees are not going away.

Carriers charge differing amounts in different situations, depending on whether the flight is domestic or international, or whether you're flying first-class or coach. Loyalty credit cards may allow for a free checked bag. In sum, the system is a minefield that will only get more spendy and is unlikely to change. Here's an example of how it works:

A family of four flies across the country with two bags per person. The first bag is charged $25 with the second charge of $35 one-way. This equals $60 per person in each direction and roundtrip adds up to $440 – likely the cost of another roundtrip ticket. Is that how you want to spend your money?

- **Check with your airline to determine the number of bags allowed and the weight restrictions for your itinerary.** To get the right answers, you need to ask the right questions whether you are speaking to a live agent or searching online.

- If you are flying on multiple carriers, **remember you are checking on your whole itinerary and all the carriers.** Regulations vary by carrier.

- **Consider not only the flights to and from your destination but also flights while at your destination.** If you are flying *to* Africa, you follow one set of rules. But when flying *within* Africa on a separate ticket, the rules may be completely different.

- Read regulations carefully on the airline web page.

- Ask questions of the airline if you have them.

Weigh the Bag at Home

It is an unnecessary stress to stand at the check-in counter, probably at some ungodly hour of the morning, worrying that your bag will exceed the weight limit. You do not want to be that person repacking your undies on the floor of the airport.

Step on your bathroom scale with the bag and without it, then subtract your body weight (your real weight, not your "goal weight") to determine how much the bag weighs. Or buy a luggage scale to avoid the math calculation.

THE TSA STYLE

Transportation Security Administration employees are there to enforce the rules. You don't have to like them, but you do have to accommodate them or spend your vacation in jail. Do it with a smile. These tips simplify the screening process.

Carry metal accessories to the airport and put them on after passing security. Or wear accessories to the airport, and **take them off before security, placing them in a Ziploc bag.** (Thank you, Peggy, for that good idea.) After collecting your items, move away from the security area to make sure you have all your belongings and to re-accessorize.

This is a good time to extol the virtues of **clear cosmetic bags**. I used to keep pencils and pens in one small bag in my large purse and lipstick in another, and I could never tell which small bag was which. Clear ones eliminate the guesswork when screeners can see the contents without having to open them.

Be a "Know It All"

Start by knowing the rules. Before you go, make sure you know the current allowances for liquids, gels, aerosols, and pastes. At this time, we are operating under the 3-1-1 plan. Each passenger is restricted to **ONE** single **one-quart bag** per person containing containers of liquids that are a 3.4-ounce size or less. You cannot take a 12-ounce bottle that contains only 3.44 ounces. I have seen many a sad lady had her expensive beauty product confiscated for not knowing that.

Even though a one-quart Ziploc bag will work, bring one that's **made of more substantial plastic. Blue Avocado makes one that** has lasted me for multiple trips. It has a flat bottom so that square-sided bottles fit in it perfectly. Because it's more durable, you won't be disposing of plastic around the world.

Here is what you need to know while going through security:

- You must show your **ID and boarding pass** to enter the security process.

- You may be required to **remove your shoes** unless you are a child or over a certain honorable age. Wear shoes that are easy to get on and off. **Wear socks** or have them to put on. Those floors where hundreds of barefooted people have walked before you give me the creeps.

- **Your computer must be removed from your bag** and placed into a TSA tub. And you could be required to turn on any electronic items.

- You must **remove all metal** from your pockets and self. This includes foil-wrapped gum, keys, coins, and CELLPHONES.

- You must **remove all outerwear including your hat.**

- Don't bring **wrapped gifts.** Security must be able to inspect what's inside.

- If you pass through a scanner, you cannot have anything on you that blocks the machine's view of your body. Carefully follow the instructions given as you approach.

- You are allowed to take many solid foods through the inspection.

- You may NOT take liquids other than those in your 3-1-1 bag.

Invest in Scottevest

The fewer items you have to carry through the security process, the easier it will be. **Scottevest** products will smooth your path. This line of functional coats and vests with multiple well-planned pockets eliminates the need for a purse, and they can be deposited easily into a TSA bin. Best of all, your possessions are available to you during takeoff and landing, as you wear the coat or vest rather than store it overhead. You can get a discount at scottevest.com/ygg by using the code YGG20 at check-out.

I cannot recommend these highly enough. The line for women is designed to flatter our figures so you will not look like you're wearing a fishing vest. The items are well-made and well-designed. I own the regular vest, lightweight vest, and trench coat and love them all.

Can I Buy You a Drink?

Buy yourself a bottle of water or fill your water bottle after you clear security. Take your own bottle to assist in eliminating plastic garbage around the world. Most airports now offer free water bottle filling stations. I appreciate their forward thinking. Before departure is when I pop an Airborne tablet into the bottle to boost my immune system before getting on the plane. When you're about to spend time in an enclosed space with other peoples' germs, it is a good to give your body a head start in the fight against them.

ON THE PLANE, TRAIN, OR BUS

Ah, you're finally settled into seat 27A, ready to spend the next chunk of your life sitting in this flying metal cylinder. Or maybe you're on a train or in the car. **Think about what you need to**

have beside you. Whether you checked your large bag or are doing the carry-on plan, you still need to have certain articles nearby for your comfort and convenience.

There are two issues to consider. ***What items do you need in transit, and what will you need if your checked bag fails to arrive with you?***

Cautionary Notes

When traveling with someone else, do what I call "cross packing." Split your things into each other's bags. If one bag is lost, each of you will still have some of your own things.

Carry essentials with you. This should include basic toiletries, all medications, and change of underwear or whatever else you cannot live without for a couple of days.

Never travel with anything of value. This includes jewelry, heirlooms, and your favorite cashmere sweater.

Laptops and other important items should never be in checked bags unless you are ready to kiss them goodbye permanently. Murphy's Law of Travel is alive and well. They will disappear.

Pack a Snack

Airplane snacks are loaded with salt, sugar, and calories. Control your choices by providing your own nutritious options such as fresh or dried fruits, vegetables, nuts, cheese, peanut butter, or jerky. Consider what you can make with just hot water from the flight attendant: soup mixes, instant oatmeal, hot chocolate, herbal tea, or even ramen noodles. (Check the nutritional value and salt content on these instant mixes; they may be inexpensive, but they also may not be healthy options.)

Once you get where you are going, if there is a big time

differential, you might find yourself hungry at inopportune times. Granola bars are handy. Remember that anything you take internationally should be packaged and not raw. Snacks eaten from the package also don't require clean hands.

Ask where to buy groceries. Especially in large cities, markets offer a variety of prepackaged salads and reasonably healthy prepared dinner and deli items. My first stop after checking into a hotel is at the closest market to stock up on snacks and picnic supplies, as well as the local flavor.

Airplane Poison

Salt, caffeine, and alcohol are your enemies on a long flight. They cause dehydration, water retention, and insomnia. Arriving at your destination with a headache and hangover does not facilitate your adjustment to a different time zone. I love wine, but it's not my friend when I fly. I limit myself to one glass and then drink a lot of my new best friend: water.

Just Plane Pretty

Wear minimal makeup for a long airplane ride. It tends to migrate to all the wrong places. You greet your destination with raccoon eyes. Apply it at journey's end. What you do need to wear is a **heavy moisturizer** containing sunscreen. Night creams do not contain SPF ingredients and hence do not protect from the UVA rays streaming through the plane's windows. Those are the rays that cause age damage to your skin. In the high altitude of the plane, you are closer to the sun, giving those rays extra impact.

Slather on lip balm with SPF while flying. Dry air, dehydration, and UV rays are unkind to kissable lips.

What Should I Wear on the Plane?

I still harbor a secret fantasy of living in the golden age of travel and descending the stairs of the plane wearing a cream-colored linen sheath, black pumps, and sexy sunglasses a la Audrey Hepburn. The coach-class crunch and pat-down security searches by strangers soon nixes this idea. What you wear needs to be functional as well as fashionable. Confident, modern women travelers must look the part.

I know from experience: It feels good to have the flight attendant refer to you as the attractive lady in seat 17C and offer to hang your coat in the first-class closet. **Dress the way you want to be treated.**

Choose something that **expands freely around the waist, stretches, doesn't wrinkle, and will survive a spilled Bloody Mary.** Thankfully, Spandex is a part of so much clothing now, including jeans. For lengthy or overnight flights, wear or change into a pair of yoga pants or leggings. But, no, please don't wear those pajama pants! You want to feel like you are in your pajamas yet look like a million bucks.

What do you do when your trip involves going through a complete change of season or climate? If you live in Michigan and travel to Mexico in March, you still want to be comfortable on both ends of the trip. Assuming it's not dangerously cold outside, leave your heavy coat in your car at the airport, or with the person who is picking you up. You can also fold up your coat once you get inside the airport. To save space, put it into a compression bag in your suitcase. Use the same concept in reverse if you are going from a warm place to a cold one: Squish down that coat, put it in the outside pocket of your bag to be accessible, and pop it out when you arrive at your chilly destination.

When rain or snow could be waiting at your destination, **pack your coat, umbrella, rain hat, gloves, and scarf** in an outside pocket of your bag for easy access. **Wear your boots** because they are too heavy to pack.

Use layering to your advantage. If you are heading out on a tropical vacation, top your sleeveless tank top with a blouse and sweater or jacket. You still may use that same sweater or jacket if the nights are cool in the tropics or the air conditioning is turned up on your cruise ship.

Cruising in Comfort and Safety at 30,000 Feet

Shoes with laces or some adjustability help if you have trouble with swelling feet. By the way, the slipper socks you sometimes are given on the plane are nice, but the soles are not solid. Do not walk into the airplane restroom in them. Invariably there is some sort of moisture on the floor, and you don't want to know what it is. A pair of solid-soled flats is better. Flip-flops, as noted earlier, are invaluable!

Sitting on an airplane is not going to be the highlight of your trip unless George Clooney is your seat mate. Business class or first class removes some of the discomfort but not all.

The first order of business is to note your seat location in relation to the emergency exits. Count the number of rows to your closest and NEXT closest exit. Read the emergency procedures. **Remove your headphones and listen politely to the flight attendant's presentation.** They are required to do it, and it won't hurt you to note any special features of your aircraft. It might hurt *not* to note them.

Leave your shoes on until you have safely completed takeoff and gained some altitude. In an emergency situation, you would need the protection for your feet. Put them back on when you begin to descend for the same reason.

Airplane seats were designed for humans shaped much

differently than most women. If your back never fits quite right in those seats, **try putting a small pillow, inflatable pillow, or folded blanket at the small of your back**. Eagle Creek makes one especially for lower back support.

Petite women may suffer as much discomfort as the 6-foot-5 man who has to bend like a pretzel to fit into his seat. **Small lifts to put under your feet** are available for purchase and may make someone with a smaller frame more comfortable. Or just use a book or your tote to achieve the same effect.

This Airplane Is Hazardous to Your Health

Deep vein thrombosis (DVT) is a SERIOUS medical threat to women travelers. Sitting or lying for long periods increases the risk of DVT. As women travelers, we are especially vulnerable. Taking estrogen or birth control pills increases the risk. For smokers, the risk grows. People over 60 are most likely to suffer from DVT, but people of *any age* can be stricken. This is what killed reporter David Bloom at age 39 in Iraq.

What is DVT? It is a condition where a blood clot forms in the body, most commonly in the legs. When the clot breaks away and migrates through the blood stream, it is called an embolism. When that clot lodges in the lungs, brain, or heart, it has the potential to cause extreme damage and death. This is not to be taken lightly or ignored.

What can we do to decrease our chance of experiencing DVT?

Assess your risk factors with the help of your doctor. If you smoke or take birth control pills or hormones, this is a particularly important discussion.

There are steps you can take to help avoid this serious condition.

- Move about the plane. Exercise in your seat and get out of your seat to walk. Some carriers even have an exercise channel or video exercise program available on demand. Do some stretches. The flight attendants need their space to serve passengers. The galley is not your gym.

- Wear compression hose. These tight-fitting socks help move the blood in your legs, improving circulation. This is a time when function trumps fashion. Rest assured. You can now find the hose in colors to match your travel outfit.

- Doctors also can prescribe effective methods of protection if you are at a high risk.

ONE WOMAN'S STORY: A CAUTIONARY TALE

She has traveled with me many times. Normally healthy and full of energy, on this trip she began having trouble breathing and complained that we were walking too far. After we walked the length of two city blocks to dinner, she wanted to take a taxi back to the hotel. She was sweating, her legs were swollen, and she had a light cough.

After two days of symptoms, I insisted she see a doctor. No one wants to take time out of a vacation to see a doctor and, like many women, this one was more comfortable as caregiver than patient. But she relented, and I accompanied her to the emergency room of an Austrian hospital.

After the initial exam and EKG, it was determined she was not having a heart attack. That was good news, but the diagnosis that followed was just as frightening: pulmonary embolism! A blood clot in her leg had traveled to her lungs. This is considered life-threatening. Thankfully, we were in the hospital, instead of at our scheduled activity, a trip to some underground salt mines. Her story ended happily, but I could have been placing a call to her family with horrible news.

Cleaning Up a Big Mess

On a long flight to India, a Bloody Mary spilled on my lap. Suddenly I was sitting in a pool of red tomato juice. I was not looking forward to the next two days with my fanny bathed in pink. The male flight attendant ran to the restroom and came back with a sanitary napkin. Holy Moses, I thought, what did he want me to do with that? He explained it was the best material for absorbing the liquid and it would not leave behind a trail of shredded white tissue and lint. He was absolutely right.

Watering from the Inside Out

Dry air in airplanes affects mucous membranes, dries skin, and can cause headaches. This leads to increased vulnerability to colds, viruses, and flu.

Drink water, and lots of it. Those plastic airline cups are too small and unstable. They force you to keep your tray table down when you'd be more comfortable with it up. Ask your flight attendant to fill your own container so that it will be available even while you sleep. Drink from it each time you awaken.

Great travel tip: An unbreakable, insulated travel cup or mug can be filled with coffee before you leave your hotel in the morning for java on the road. When staying at an all-inclusive resort, have the bartender make your drink in it so that you have a container for the pool or beach. On the plane you can use it for water.

FACT: Lack of sleep exacerbates jet lag and plays havoc with your immune system. Even when traveling between north and south, a sleep deficit will sneak up on you.

SOLUTION: Get a good night's sleep before departure. Check with your doctor about an appropriate sleep aid. Homeopathic remedies such as NoJetLag and melatonin or Tylenol PM may be effective. Whatever you choose, be sure to try it at home in advance to monitor your reaction.

FACT: Aches and pains can be a barrier to sleeping en route.

SOLUTION: Check with your medical professional about **taking an analgesic or anti-inflammatory medication BEFORE departing.** They might be beneficial to control little pains before they become big pains.

FACT: Pressurized airplane cabins cause bloating, gas, and irregularity.

SOLUTION: Beside drinking plenty of water, eat **healthy food choices containing fiber.** Check with your doctor for how best to handle bloating, gas, and irregularity. Some people carry bran or flax seeds to add to their breakfast. Others need more serious help.

BYOB and More

BYOB means **Bring Your Own Blanket** on planes now. The **CoolMax blanket** folds up to be quite small and is very light. On a recent car trip, I took mine and wore it as a shawl too, because it draped so softly and was such a pretty color. Your pashmina or shawl can serve the same function.

I never leave home without an **inflatable pillow.** Eagle Creek makes one with a plush covering that breathes, unlike the less expensive plastic pillows. Your inflatable pillow can also be used to plump up a hotel pillow; inflate to the desired firmness and stick it underneath the bed pillow. Avoid the ones full of little pellets. They take up too much space and are one more thing to carry.

A good **eyeshade or mask** is as important as the pillow. If, like me, you need to shut out the light in order to sleep, this addition will be useful on the plane as well as when your roommate wants to read, write, or watch TV.

THE CAR TRIP

Pack light and plan ahead just like for a plane trip. Here are some additional issues to consider when planning a road trip:

Who gets to choose? The rule in my

marriage is that the **driver decides the temperature and the music.** Unless you enjoy hours of Bruce Springsteen (my husband's choice on the radio), take your own music source and headphones.

Take a blanket to keep you warm, even in summer. Air conditioning blowing on your legs can make you miserable. Take the same inflatable pillow you'd use on the plane, either to grab a nap or to give your back lumbar support. The **eye mask and earplugs** are useful, too.

The **tote bag** is an equally important asset in the car. It keeps your maps, mints, coffee mug, binoculars, and other necessities close at hand.

An **ice chest stores cold beverages**, carries healthy snacks, and ensures my wine bottle will be chilled when we reach our destination. When I travel by car or rail in Europe, I take a fold-up cooler that fits in my luggage and can be used to pack a picnic.

RENTAL CARS

Renting a car gives you the freedom to get off the beaten track and flexibility to do it on your own schedule. However, this also opens up another level of decision-making to match your needs to the best car options. Here are some considerations.

- **How important is comfort?** If you're driving long distances for many days, a comfortable, quiet vehicle might be your priority.

- **Rentals are expensive,** so rent for the shortest time possible. The exception is that there might be a weekly or monthly rate that will save you money over the daily rate. Rentals are in 24-hour increments. If you pick up at 9 a.m.

and drop off three days later at 2 p.m., you pay for a whole 4th day. Ouch!

- **Where are you going?** In countries where car theft is a huge problem, including Eastern Europe and South America, rental companies will not allow you to take their cars into certain other countries. They also may exclude some specific routes they consider too dangerous, such as the road beyond the Mauna Kea Visitor Information Station on the island of Hawaii.

- **Where do you want to pick up and drop off?** You can assume that airport, downtown, and suburban locations have different costs. Airports usually levy a surcharge. Beware of the fees for a one-way rental. That could be expressed as a drop off fee or a higher overall rate.

- **What size car do you need?** How many passengers and how much luggage do you have? Soft-sided bags pack more easily than hard. Rent a large car if driving a small one on the Autobahn is going to scare you. Just remember that streets overseas are narrow, and gas can be prohibitively expensive. I've seen fuel for $1 per gallon in Dubai and $8 in Switzerland.

- **What style car do you need?** Can you drive a stick shift? They can be less expensive. And if you're hauling odd-shaped items, such as bicycles or surfboards, maybe you need a roof carrier or a station wagon. Wagons and hatchbacks hold more, but you sacrifice some security. Your personal items might be exposed.

- **Where does your insurance take you?** Your U.S. auto insurance probably does not follow you to another country. If you pay for a rental with certain credit cards, you may have some coverage. Check with your insurance carrier and credit card supplier before you go: Taking a chance could be costly and dangerous.

- **Do you need a GPS?** This can be a lifesaver if you know how to use one or are willing to learn. You can rent them from most car rental companies or take your own portable device. Be sure you have the most recent program loaded in it. If you rent one, confirm that it is guaranteed to be in English or a language you understand.

- **Are there parking issues you need to contend with?** Does your hotel offer parking and what is its cost? Is it secured? How do you reach it? Sometimes it is not onsite but blocks away. And, in big cities all over the world, parking is a problem. You might be better off using public transportation there.

Great travel tip: Gas in countries using the metric system is quoted per liter; multiply by four to get the approximate per-gallon rate.

Picking up Your Car

The language of car rental insurance is confusing. Consult your travel agent about a **prepaid rate;** this will save you money and give you the chance to consider your options in advance. Before you take possession of the car, inspect it carefully. Take a good look all the way around it to **note any possible damage**. Call any questionable damage to the attention of the rental agent, and take a photo to document it.

And You Are Off

- **Have maps or navigation tools ready**. A good co-pilot is indispensable, and a bad one is a nightmare. Just ask my husband.

- **Have change ready for toll roads**. You will need local currency. The tollbooth is not an exchange service, although some do take credit cards. Note whether there's a line for drivers with a prepaid pass or who are making an electronic payment. Don't worry if you get in the wrong line or make a mistake. Yes, the guy behind you may honk at you but try to remain calm and unflustered. It is dangerous to suddenly reverse or U-turn. Someone will come out to help you if you are confused or in the wrong place. It is a learning experience. You will catch on.

- **Co-piloting is easier with binoculars.** If this sounds a bit silly, try them and see: Sometimes those signs come up on you quickly. It never hurts to have "an extra pair of good eyes."

Putting on the Dog or Catting Around

Our dog takes road trips with us, and sometimes the cat does, too. It adds a new level of complications and responsibility.

- **Schedule plenty of potty stops** for people and puppies. Provide a **small litter box** for the cat.

- **Plan meal stops** considering that pets cannot be left in a hot car.

- **Keep animals in a proper pet carrier** to prevent them from running away when you stop.

- **List your home phone and cell phone** number on the pet's ID tag. You aren't home, are you?

- **Have your pet mircochipped** to help you reunite if it is lost.

- **Know the documentation requirements** if you are crossing borders. One of our first family trips with a dog was into Canada, which has regulations requiring special documentation for our four-legged friends. Additionally, if you are taking pets (by boat or plane) to Hawaii, note the very strict regulations for importing pets.

CRUISE SHIP TIPS

Whether you are preparing for your first cruise or are a returning guest, these tips ensure a bon voyage!

Cruise lines have loyalty programs. Each time you cruise on the same line, you get closer to upgrades, shipboard credits and other amenities. Not unlike the airlines' frequent flyer programs, most automatically keep track of your bookings, although I know of at least one that requires passengers to register. Check to make sure you receive credit for past voyages.

Cruise ships are a cashless society. When you embark, you present your credit card, which is held on file, and receive a cruise ID for security and to log extra charges for such amenities as shore excursions, boutique purchases, spa services, and drinks from the bar. When you disembark, the amount owing can be paid in cash or charged to your credit card. Gratuity policies vary, so check when you book your cruise; some add them automatically and others ask that an envelope of cash be given directly to the room steward or waiter.

- **Take a copy of the cruise brochure.** It will have a good deck plan which can be hard to come by onboard. It contains other helpful miscellaneous details as well.

- **A small handbag** is the best means for carrying your cruise card and any other personal items around the ship and ashore. Get one with a long strap so you can carry it as a cross-body bag. This frees your hands to grab the stair railing or casino chips, and to get on and off tenders safely. Tenders are those smaller boats that may be used in some ports to ferry you ashore.

- Public rooms of ships are cold, freezing cold, even in the tropics. **Take a sweater, jacket, or wrap.** You will need one for evenings in the dining room, casino and showrooms, as well as for more casual activities, such as the movie theater.

- **Pay attention to the number of formal nights.** Many lines are yielding to sentiment (mostly from men) against them. Check whether you need to take formal wear at all. While I mourn the change, it sure makes packing easier.

- **Be very careful on cruises**, whether you are traveling alone, with a friend, or with a partner. You must remain as vigilant as you are anywhere else. There is no background screening for your fellow passengers. Keep an eye on your drink, and don't overindulge. Don't visit anyone's stateroom or invite someone to yours. Even the staff doesn't always have your best interests at heart. The people serving you are often from other cultures. They are working for tips. Beware of the potential for cultural misunderstandings.

CHAPTER 8

Finances

Whether IT'S YOUR VACATION OR
your retirement, your travel time is precious. And
so are your travel dollars. Very few of us can
throw caution to the wind and travel and spend
at will. Money matters weigh heavily on our
minds as we plan and execute our plans.

TRAVEL AND LIFE DECISIONS

For years, I discounted the value of travel insurance. But
after traveling as much as I have, I've become a convert.

Be certain you **understand the cancellation penalties** surrounding your trip. Once you are aware of them you are likely to
want to consider purchasing travel insurance. It gives you a sense of
security in case of an emergency. It feels good to know there is an
entity standing behind you. Having that toll-free number in your
purse gives you an added aura of protection. Your travel agent will
help you obtain this coverage.

Here is a primer on the basics of travel insurance. Note,

however, that each policy differs, and every situation brings its own set of facts. These are only the basics.

The four primary components of the policy are trip cancellation, trip interruption, emergency medical evacuation, and medical coverage.

- **The cancellation portion protects you from losing the money already paid in the event you cannot take the trip.** The reasons covered normally include illness, injury or death - yours, your travel partner's, or certain members of your family.

- **Trip interruption** protects you if you cannot complete your trip after it has begun.

- **Emergency evacuation returns you home if you become ill or injured while on your trip.** Evacuation from your safari via helicopter and private plane, would blow anyone's travel budget. This aspect of the policy is very important, especially if you travel far or to a remote area. Activities such as scuba and skydiving are not usually covered, but a broken back from diving into the ocean probably is.

- **Medical coverage** is the option that pays for medical treatment not covered by your primary health insurance. Generally, your health insurance doesn't follow you abroad. This medical coverage is usually secondary to any other insurance that may apply.

- **Lost luggage and travel delay** coverage are also included as small additional benefits of most policies.

I have had my share of times when such insurance was

sorely - and I mean sorely - needed: dental emergencies, an emergency appendectomy on an Antarctic cruise, a broken back in Hawaii, a broken arm and a heart attack in the Costa Rican cloud forest, and a blood pressure crisis in Austria. Because no one is invincible, **spend the little extra for the peace of mind and protection of pocketbook it brings.**

Chances are that you will return from your trip safe and sound. But, while on the subject of planning for emergencies, I suggest you prepare for your trip by addressing other serious adult matters, such as **making or updating your will.** Leave town with the knowledge that you are prepared for every contingency.

Provide access to your online accounts and the associated passwords to someone you trust, or tell that person where such information can be found. There are programs or apps that will handle this if you are comfortable using them.

MONEY MATTERS

Financial questions are among the first thing I'm asked by prospective travelers. How much will this trip cost? How will I pay for items I buy en route? How do I obtain cash on the road? How can I save money? Sit down with a cup of tea; we have a lot of questions to cover.

Save Money Before You Leave

Budgeting never goes on vacation – at least, not for most of us. Here are some effective ways to stretch your dollars:

- **Plan ahead** to avoid expediting fees and charges for last-minute bookings. This also applies to clothing and other purchases made especially for your trip.

- Shop smart. **Dollar Stores** are a good place to find toothbrushes, toiletries, washcloths, slippers, over-the-counter medications, and much more. My most recent treasure from this chain was a package of daytime and nighttime cold medication for $1.

- **Travel off-season, shoulder season and midweek** to get off to a thrifty start. If you have vacationed in low season, you no doubt appreciated the smaller crowds at popular sites. The Mona Lisa is just as haunting in January as in July.

- **When choosing your accommodations, look carefully at the meal options.** If you don't rise in time to eat the included breakfast, you've wasted money by paying for it. There is usually an option to *not* include breakfast. If you are traveling with teenagers or big eaters, then consider a partial or all-inclusive meal plan.

- **Make your own breakfast**. Granola bars, instant oatmeal, cereal, pastry, juice, and fruit are easy to manage on your own. We tend to think picnics are for lunch, but why not "picnic" for breakfast in your hotel room? Bring items from home or purchase them at a local market. If your room has a refrigerator, you are really in business.

- **Hotel taxes and fees can be substantial.** Know what is included in the quote and what will be added. Some fees to look out for are the value-added tax (VAT), resort fees, occupancy fees, and city taxes. With cruises, be aware of all the taxes, port charges, and the tipping policy.

- **Seek out "value-added" packages.** For example, in Southern California or Florida, your hotel may include admission to theme parks and attractions. Some hotels offer laundry service, parking, or breakfast. Chains like Kimpton and Embassy Suites include an evening wine or cocktail hour. Cruise lines may include gratuities, shore excursions, or shipboard credits. These all carry a value.

THRIFTSHOP, THROW AWAY, BEG, OR BORROW

Thriftshop

Need a Hawaiian shirt in January? How about a specialty item, such as a safari vest, or cowboy shirt? **Check out your neighborhood thrift or consignment shop.** Many of these outlets support local charities, so your spending supports your community and saves you money. When you return home and no longer need the item, pass it on to another traveler or **donate it back** to the thrift shop for someone else to use on her next trip. Win, win, win!

My Dirty Secret

Pack clothes that are ready to be retired. Throw them out on your trip and make room for some wonderful souvenir. In my travels I've left behind underwear, an old dress, ragged nightgowns, boots past their prime, and a stretched-out bathing suit. Just make sure you tell the front desk that you intend to leave the items behind so they aren't retrieved from the trash and returned to you. You can also leave discards at the reception desk and let the staff determine whether they should be thrown away or can find a new life locally.

Beg or Borrow

Borrowing is a wonderful way to save money on things you may just need to use only once. I have been happy to lend specialty items such as luggage, electric converters, and travel irons. Just remember to bring them back in good condition - accompanied, I advise, by a small treat for the lender.

THIS IS GONNA COST YA
How Much Will It Cost?

The airfare and hotel costs are easy to calculate, but the add-ons add up. An easy tool is to break all costs down to a **per-person, per-day rate.** Here are guidelines for compiling the foreseeable costs, including lodging, meals, activities, transportation (subway, taxi, water taxi), and shopping. Gratuities should be included, as they can be considerable, especially on a cruise.

- Hotel: Divide the nightly room rate by the number of guests per room to get the per person rate per night. Rates usually are quoted per room and not per person. Include all taxes, service, and resort fees.

- Meals: Include days in transit to and from your destination. Be realistic. Beyond breakfast, lunch and dinner, what snacks and drinks should you plan on? Cruises generally charge for non-alcoholic drinks because they come from the bar and because they can do so.

- Activities: Entertainment costs add up quickly, especially if your taste is for operas, Broadway shows, Disneyland, or guided tours.

- Transportation: Subway, bus, taxi, and airport shuttles fares factor in here.

- Tipping: This can be a considerable expense and in many cases needs to be tendered in cash. It is proper to pay in local currency or the currency of your vessel, in the case of a cruise. The cruise or tour brochure or website will outline the policies.

- Shopping: Set a budget at the beginning to prevent overspending. For budgeting purposes, you can account for it as a total amount or a daily cost.

CURRENCY Q&A

In what form should I carry money?

Which should I take: U.S. dollars, local currency, credit cards, debit cards, or travelers' checks? The answer could be – all of the above. But how much and in what form depends on how many of your costs are prepaid, where you are going, and what you expect to spend when you get there.

U.S. Dollars

Obviously, if you are traveling in the U.S., you will be using dollars. Abroad you may have some small use for them on the way there and back for tipping, meals, and some transportation.

The USD is a desirable currency in some countries, but not many. Overall, it is best to use local currency to avoid drawing attention as a foreigner. However, dollars may be able to get you out of a jam, in which case remember: **A $100 U.S. bill speaks louder than five $20 bills.** I call that **BIG PROBLEM, BIG MONEY.**

In places such as Ecuador and Laos where dollars are used widely, be aware that sometimes bills in denominations of $50s or larger are not readily accepted. Bills not in perfect condition are

Accounting For Your Trip

Pretend you've planned a 10-day trip, with five nights on land and four on a ship. The cruise portion is prepaid, but the following expenses are what remain. **These numbers are fictitious and intended only to show you how to plan your travel budget.**

Hotel
$200 per night/2 guests= $100 per night per person, 5 nights......... $500

Lunches
Included on cruise; on land, 6 @ $15 each................................90

Dinners
Included on cruise, dinners on land 6 @ $40......................240

Snacks and Drinks
Snacks.. 100
Half-bottle of wine with dinner, one beer for lunch, one
cocktail, $20 + $5 + $10 = 10 days @ $35............................350

Activities
Shore excursions and activities: $150 per day x 4 = $600
Museums and activities on land: $40 per day x 6 = $240.............840

Transportation
Taxi to airport: $40
Subway pass: $125
Bus tickets 4 x $3 = $12
Shuttle bus to airport on departure: $75 252

Tipping
On cruise: waiter, room steward for 4 days @ $10/day 40

Shopping
Holiday gifts: $200
Treats for me: $400
Gift for pet sitter: $50...650

Meals in transit
Lunch, wine, snack each way, $40 x 2 80

TOTAL (minus cruise cost) ....$3,042 difficult to negotiate. You can request new bills from your bank with enough notice.

Local currency is the tried and true choice. Since most countries in Europe have converted to the euro, they do not take the pre-euro currencies such as francs, shillings, and pesetas. Don't drag out your old collection of those.

As the exchange rate fluctuates, you receive more or less foreign currency for your money. An overseas traveler from the U.S. gets a bargain if the dollar has a high value, not so much when the dollar's value falls.

Some items are a good value in one country over another but for reasons other than the currency rate. Coffee in Costa Rica may be less expensive because it is grown there. Alcoholic beverages are expensive in Sweden because they are heavily taxed. Food is expensive in the Caribbean because it is imported. Goods are more expensive in states with a high sales tax and in countries with a high value-added tax (VAT).

What the heck is VAT and what's this I hear about a refund of it?

This is unfamiliar territory for U.S. citizens. The simplistic explanation is that the value-added tax (VAT) is similar to a national sales tax. It is *included* in the purchase price when you buy something. Many countries have a VAT, and the rates differ.

Sometimes your receipt will show the breakdown of the item and VAT, but the price on the item still includes it. However, when you book a hotel, be sure it is included.

In Europe, Canada, Japan, and Australia, non-residents may be eligible for **a VAT refund.** Each country has its own set of rules but, generally speaking, you must have made a large purchase, and when you depart the country, you need to present the item, the original receipt, and a form to the VAT refund office in the airport. This may well be worth jumping through the hoops if you have made a large purchase. Ask the merchant who made the sale or search online to obtain the details that fit your specific situation. If you have shipped goods home, you can still be entitled to the refund, but shipping costs may offset the savings.

How do I exchange money before I leave?

When traveling abroad, **obtain some local currency** before departure. You don't know if and when you'll be able to exchange money on arrival. You may need it right away for transportation or tips. More importantly, you don't want to spend the first two days of your vacation searching for the best exchange rate. Avoid the airport exchange; rates there are usually terrible.

Bank hours and holidays are not the same around the world. Cover the members of your party for about two days' worth of expenses in local currency. Don't expect to get the rate you see posted online or in the newspaper. You will pay a premium. Banks and currency exchange services are the main sources for exchanging money at home. Check also with your credit union, travel agent, or auto club office.

The local branch of your bank probably will not have foreign currency on hand, but they can order it with enough advance notice.

Companies such as **Travelex** have brick-and-mortar locations. They are helpful and offer a variety of products and services. Travelex, **Oanda, and Forex** also offer currency delivered to your door within a few days.

When you exchange money at home, you'll normally receive it all as paper bills and no coins. Often the first

Great travel tip:
The smallest paper denomination of a euro is a $5 euro note. The $1 and $2 euros are coins.

amounts you will need are small ones so you will want some coins. Stop in an airport shop and buy a candy bar to break a bill for tipping the restroom attendant.

On your return, you will not be able to exchange coins back into dollars. Buy a treat in the duty-free shop, put them in your scrapbook or give them to the charity that collects change in the airport or on the plane home.

Great travel tip: Toss the leftover currency into an envelope or Ziploc bag for use on the next trip. Or give it to a friend visiting the same destination.

What is my money worth?

You have cash in hand and head off to the market. Right off, a potential purchase catches your eye. Performing the arithmetic to convert money on the spot is difficult even for the best math student. Given your jet lag and the challenges of coping in a strange place, your orderly thinking goes out the tent flap.

The currency will become easier to deal with as you go. But until then, try one of these ideas to help.

- **Find an easy mnemonic device.** If the exchange rate is 1.42 to the dollar, add the full amount in dollars and add one-half. So $300 becomes 300 + 150 or $450. That gets you close enough to knowing the cost in dollars, but even that can be hard when you're tired.

- **Put your cell phone to use**. There are plenty of free conversion applications, or use the calculator function.

- To be more discreet, **make a conversion chart** to carry in your pocket. I laminate mine or cover it in wide clear tape. Sites such as Oanda's provide free charts to print at home.

Great travel tip: A coin purse with sections or a pouch with multiple zippers will keep your yen (Japanese currency) separated from your baht (Thai currency).

How Do I Get Cash?

You don't want to *carry* the cash you need for your whole trip. So what are your options? Your hotel might offer exchange services, as do banks, currency exchanges, and ATMs, with ATMs usually being the preferred.

Exchange money only through appropriate channels. Black market transactions are not worth the risk. NEVER, EVER exchange money on the street, with a stranger, or on the black market. You may end up with counterfeit bills and/or in jail.

How about the ATM?

You can readily obtain local currency at ATMs around the world **by using your 4-digit PIN.** International ATMs do NOT have letter keys, only numbers. Be sure you know your PIN as numbers and not letters.

Exchange rates are usually the best at the ATM, but there may be an "out of network" transaction fee of about $5, making it better to **withdraw a single large amount than multiple smaller ones.** There also could be a small transaction fee that is a percentage of the amount withdrawn.

Most banks are part of a network of partner banks that may forgive the transaction fee. Find out which, if any, are in your network, and whether there is a flat or percentage fee for conversion. **Call your bank or search its website to clarify the costs of in-network or out-of-network transactions before you go.**

Should I bring travelers' checks?

Short answer – no. Because of counterfeiting schemes, many merchants no longer accept travelers' checks. They are becoming difficult to purchase. Their major advantages were as a back-up in a failure of the electronic banking system, their easy of replacement if lost or stolen, and that you did not necessarily need a bank to exchange them. The disadvantage is that they are no longer widely accepted. I do not carry them and would say that you should not run out to get them.

Great travel tip:
Don't flash cash as it comes out of the ATM. Count it and immediately put it in a safe place. Be alert to your surroundings.

What about a credit card cash advance?

Avoid cash advances on your credit card. They are very expensive. Interest starts compounding immediately, and they carry huge fees. This is an option only for dire emergencies.

What about foreign currency prepaid debit cards?

These are a recent offering. They have names like the Chip and PIN Cash Passport, available from Travelex. They are available in only a few currencies. Advantages are that they offer the safety and convenience of a credit card; the downside is that they are preloaded with a set amount you determine, requiring you to keep track of your spending like a debit card. The exchange rate is not as good as using an ATM. You can add funds to the card remotely if you have access to the Internet. **But be careful about banking from a computer that may not be secure.**

What do you know about currency exchanges on the road?

Those exchanges you see on the street are the worst bargains around. The rate posted on the sign outside is NOT what you will end up receiving. They pile on fee after fee. It is best to avoid them.

What's the best way to spend money?

The world is changing. I just encountered for the first time, stores in Amsterdam that do not accept cash. Payment had to be made with a credit card or debit card with PIN. This new development helps eliminate theft by employees and robbery by criminals. It is cleaner for employees to not handle unclean money near food, and it saves time in the payment process – or so I was told. My usual response has been to say **cash is king**, but maybe now it is only a prince!

Local currency is still preferred over U.S. dollars in most places. Plus: **Discounts are often available when you pay in cash.** If you're bargaining, you must pay in cash. The price you negotiate goes out the window or market stall when you bring out the plastic. Merchants pay a percentage to process credit cards, and that cuts directly into their bottom line.

Cash is especially appropriate for small transactions or in a market where small independent vendors don't accept credit cards.

Credit Cards

Debit or credit cards work well for hotels, meals in restaurants, or large purchases. They are easy and safe to use. The following will help you use them with intelligence and safety.

Inform your bank when you plan to travel, even domestically. This applies to your credit and debit cards. Carry at least two cards in the event there is an issue with one of them. Two debit cards and two credit cards should be sufficient backup.

Has your bank's fraud department ever called you to confirm charges on your credit card? What if they begin questioning legitimate charges on your card from Bali, where you're vacationing there? Banking problems eat up valuable time and can require expensive overseas phone calls at off hours. I've informed my bank of my plans and still had a problem. Nothing is certain in this world. Be happy the bank is watching out for you.

Make copies of the front and back of your cards and take them with you. Carry them separately from where you keep your cards. I enlarge my copy to clarify the critical phone numbers on the back; those are ones to call if the card is missing. Normally you can fit several on one page. To save bulk (and trees), use the front and back of the paper. Scanning or photographing is also an option.

The paper trail of a credit card is helpful for tracking expenses. The disadvantage is the possibility of loss or theft.

Check with your card providers before departure for fees on foreign transactions. There is usually a fee in the 1 to 3 percent range for use of credit cards abroad. They vary enough to make it worthwhile to check the differences. Visa and MasterCard are widely accepted, but American Express can be iffy. Discover and Diner's Club generally are not useful internationally.

Debit Cards

Your debit card with Visa or Mastercard affiliation should be accepted as such. Remember that most rental car companies do not accept debit cards.

Chip Cards

Outside the U.S., credit cards come with a chip imbedded in the card, a system that credit card companies in this country are now adopting. This provides a much higher level of security. In most places merchants still accept cards with a magnetic strip. However, for most ticket vending machines in Europe, you need a chip card. If you don't have one, you go to the ticket window and buy your ticket from an attendant.

It is common in foreign restaurants that they bring the chip card reader right to you table. This eliminates the risk of having your card leave your sight. It is a good thing.

TIPPING

Tipping policies around the world could fill a book of their own. Giving gratuities is complicated and very personal. Rest assured that almost anyone who provides a service is on the list of those who expect to be tipped. These include guides, drivers, maids, waiters, room stewards, wine stewards, room service delivery, concierges, and a host of others. Books, the Internet, your travel agent, or your tour operator can guide you through this minefield.

Your research should include other charges that may surprise you, such as there being a table fee or being charged for what you take out of the breadbasket. Always **check your restaurant bill to see whether or not a gratuity was added.** In many places outside the U.S., it is added automatically. It may appear as an addition on the bottom of the bill, or in some cases, it may not. Check the menu to see if the gratuity policy is spelled out. It is usually noted near the bottom of the page someplace in small print.

I am finding many **restaurants at home and**

Great travel tip: Be considerate by tipping in local currency.

abroad asking that tips be tendered in cash. This is not a scam but, rather, an attempt to make sure the server is directly paid and not cheated out of the tip by a higher-up who pockets the money he or she rightfully deserves.

Pack a stack of U.S. $1 bills. They are just what you need for tipping at home or in transit when traveling internationally. PLEASE don't use them to tip for services abroad. The recipient has to take them to a bank and loses money in the exchange.

SAVING ON THE ROAD

Here are some ways to control your costs when you are away from home. Some of them will add a dose of fun you may not have expected.

Food

Eat your large meal at lunch. Lunches out are less expensive than dinners.

Stay in a condominium or apartment. Especially in resort areas such as Hawaii, Mexico, and Palm Springs, a condo is a good option for families or anyone wishing to cook some or all of their own meals. Apartment rentals are becoming popular all over the world with resources such as Airbnb.

Choose a hotel with a microwave and/or refrigerator. You can cook a small meal and store food items. It is usually okay to empty the mini-bar to store your own food. Just remember to carefully return the hotel's items so you don't get charged for them.

Look for restaurants with **early dining specials or prix fixe menus.** They are displayed on an outside blackboard in Europe. **Leave the busy**

Great travel tip: Do not be led astray by strangers approaching you to promote their restaurant or their cousin's shop.

touristy streets and check out local neighborhoods. Ask the hotel's staff or other locals you meet for affordable suggestions of restaurants and neighborhoods. They live there. They know!

To avoid the embarrassment of sitting down in a restaurant and discovering the cost is beyond your budget, **check the menu first.** Restaurants in most countries post them at the entrance. If you're in a place that doesn't, asking to see a menu before sitting down is a perfectly acceptable practice. A polite thank you will suffice if you decide against being seated.

In France It Is a Pique Nique

Some of my most memorable meals on the road have been picnics, on the train, in the car, in a park, or at my hotel. Making a meal that can be enjoyed in your hotel room is a relaxing way to end a busy day. Supermarkets sell small bags of lettuce for an easy salad. Farmers' markets offer vegetables, fruits, and local seasonal specialties. Use dinner shopping as an opportunity to mix with locals and to get closer to the food sources.

Pack plates, napkins, and utensils. I have given up paper plates for a set of reusable, lightweight plastic plates from the Dollar Store, along with a small cutting board. I can whip up quite a meal on the road. The people at To-Go Ware make a nice set of bamboo utensils in a carrying case. It includes a knife, folk, spoon, and chopsticks! They are just what you need to set a perfect picnic table. No plastic in the landfill and no metal to set off security alarms. If you are serious about picnics, toss in **a bit of dishwashing soap and perhaps a sponge.**

My most recent treasure is To-Go Ware's collapsible silicone bowl with a lid that seals well. You can make a salad or bowl of cereal or soup in it. It is also wonderful for storing leftovers. Pop those leftover picnic olives in it tonight and take them on the train for lunch tomorrow. It is light and takes very little space.

And remember the corkscrew! It is supposed to be permitted in your carry-on if it doesn't have a foil cutter blade – although a TSA agent may feel otherwise, so take one you are willing to lose.

I also keep a **Haley's Corker** in my picnic bag. It acts to aerate, filter, pour, re-cork and stop up any wine bottle. Drink part of a bottle of wine, stick in the Haley, and pop it in your carry-on bag for your lunch the next day. This wine winner can be found in kitchen and wine shops or at www.winecorker.org.

Bring **plastic bags to store leftover picnic supplies** in the fridge.

That **small, soft-sided cooler** you packed is going to come in handy now.

Sleeping

Lodging is one of the biggest expenses of any trip. For my money, it's a good value to choose a hotel close to the sights you came to see and in a safe area. Before you decide to stay farther away to save money, calculate the additional cost of getting to and from your activities. Consider these other questions to save on hotels:

- Is a better view worth the additional cost?

- Does the hotel offer a multiple-night discount or reduced weekend/weekday rate?

- Can you save with a prepaid, non-refundable rate (assuming you have confidence in your plans)?

- What membership discounts does the hotel honor (in the U.S., typically such groups as the military, AARP, and AAA)?

- How many of you are sharing the room? How many are allowed in the room? Traveling solo carries extra costs on tours and cruises. **Most tour companies and cruise lines offer a share plan.** My own You Go Girls! does this. If you have a little adventure in you, choose to share a room, make a friend and save some money.

Cleaning – Dry or Otherwise

Laundry service in your hotel will be expensive, unless you're in India. Save money by doing your own or finding the **local laundromat or cleaners.** Allow enough turnaround time and remember to pick up your items before you leave town. Launder like a local!

Shopping

The late Suzy Gershman, author of the "Born to Shop" series, originated the "Moscow Rule of Shopping:" Most people want to shop around for the best deal. That behavior makes sense in most situations. But if you live in Moscow, where goods are often scarce, you must grab an item as soon as you see it. This maxim is true when you travel. You seldom have the luxury of comparison shopping. So if it's not some souvenir that's available everywhere, the source is reputable, and the quality is good, grab it and don't look back.

Get comfortable with bargaining. In many places, haggling over price is an age-old practice. If you haven't bargained before, start learning. Your first offer should be about 30 per cent under the asking price. Then go from there with an ultimate goal in your mind. Be prepared to walk away if you are not

Great travel tip: If you buy books abroad, make sure you are getting an English copy.

agreeing. The price often makes a bounce in your favor if you are willing to leave without a deal. If you're buying a number of items from the same merchant, your negotiating power is stronger. Aim to get one of the items thrown in for free. Bargaining is deeply ingrained in some cultures. I know a person whose doctor called *him* to offer a lower surgery price.

Save money, weight, and space in your luggage by not purchasing books in museum shops. Instead, write down the title or take a photograph of the cover and purchase them online from the comfort of your own home. Occasionally you are not be able to find them at your regular source, but usually you can.

Sightseeing

Museum passes and free museum days can be money savers. Major museums list the free entrance times on their websites.

Passes such as the British Heritage Pass and the Paris Museum Pass not only save money but also time and hassles. They eliminate waiting in long lines to purchase tickets for each visit. Make sure you assess your tolerance level before purchasing such a pass, because you have to visit a good number of museums to get the bargain. Divide the number of exhibitions you want to see into the cost to find the cost per use.

For example, if the current cost of a Paris Museum Pass is $91 for four days, you'd need to visit two museums every day for four days to make the pass pay for itself. Or, if you only average one museum each day, is it worth the price to avoid waiting in line for tickets and admission? With most passes, you must use the multi-day variety on consecutive days.

Likewise, with **rail or bus passes.** They are not automatically a good investment. Sometimes point-to-point fares are the better value. If you purchase a subway pass for $40 and use it only four times, it's not a good deal.

When you buy a tour, **check to see if there is another one that pairs with it.** When you take the morning City Tour, check for an afternoon tour that you can add. There is usually a discount for taking two tours back-to-back.

Seek out walking tours. The fact that no vehicle is involved in a walking tour clearly saves a lot of money. Locals with a passion for their subject often conduct such tours, and some are even licensed guides. Just be careful to stick with tours put on by actual tour companies or tourist bureaus, not by a random person who approaches you to offer his or her services. I can vouch for Pariswalks and Londonwalks as both being professional and very reasonable. Tours by Locals is also a good resource to check.

CHAPTER 9

Time Travel

All ANY OF US REALLY HAVE IN THIS WORLD is time. It is our most valuable resource and yet we don't even know how much of it we have. How we spend it and how we waste it make our lives what they are. Let's deal with all things related to time.

GET YOUR HEAD TOGETHER

Stress increases susceptibility to illness. So give yourself some wiggle room. Set a goal to be ready the day before your actual departure. Ideally, clear your schedule for the entire day before you depart. This doesn't mean deceiving your friends or employer, and I am *certainly* not suggesting that you can prepare for your trip in a single day. The idea is that you need space to deal with any of the last-minute issues that invariably arise. Having everything in order gives you time to recharge yourself for the trip ahead.

I was pretty much ready for a long trip to Europe when a torn retina threw a wrench into my week. The laser repair and follow-up

Great travel tip:
To start on your way with confidence, be ready a day ahead of departure, and get a good night's sleep. A completed to-do list is as good as a sleeping pill.

visit took two days out of my pre-trip preparation. Then a last-minute houseguest arrived the night before my departure. Rather than miss time with my friend, I simply excused myself for an early bedtime. Eye repaired, friend enjoyed, and off to Europe. Stuff happens, and it can happen to you.

It is natural to experience a mixture of excitement and anxiety before a trip. There is wonderful anticipation over the coming new experiences, but there also can be anxiety over not knowing what to expect. You are normal to feel some anxiety.

WORLD TIME

As you make your way around the world you will soon find that not everyone shares the same urgency with regard to being on time and keeping appointments. It is manifested in fellow travelers who do not respect time limits – you know the ones - they are always the last one onto the bus or to meet in the hotel lobby. They are always just a bit late. And that is why you will always **know what your time commitments are and meet them.** It is one thing to miss out on your own appointments, but there is another person on the other side of that agreement who is hurt by your rude behavior.

Now comes a tricky part. **Not all cultures honor time in the same way.** In many places it is customary to be late. Time is just a suggestion to be accepted when it works out. In some places that is known as the "mañana culture," in others it is simply a disregard for time without a label. These are cultural norms that you are not going to change. If you are on time, you will never have a problem, but be aware that you may have to wait patiently for the other person. When interacting with locals, such as having dinner in their home, find out what the expectation is for being on time. In the Philippines for example, it is rude to arrive at the appointed time for dinner.

THE WAITING GAME

The privilege of travel inevitably brings with it the punishment of waiting. Much of that waiting revolves around transportation. Time is spent waiting for planes, trains, and boats. But there is also the wait for your hotel room to be ready, your luggage to be delivered to your cruise stateroom, and waiting in line for museums and attractions. Waiting and more waiting is a recipe for frustration.

While the root of the waiting may be out of your control, you can control your reaction. Smart travelers spin that time into a positive.

Adopt a "Waitful" Attitude

You know those waits are coming. Commit to not let them ruin your spirits. They are just a small surcharge on your admission ticket to the world. Would you let that keep you at home? This definitely falls into the category of a "first world problem."

Make Plans

You know you are going to have time on your hands so-BYOE (Bring Your Own Entertainment). Crossword puzzles and Sudokus stretch your brain and speed waiting times. Purchase them in books, download them, play them online, or cut them out of the daily newspaper. Then use that mechanical pencil you packed, unless you are one of those who does the New York Times Sunday Crossword in ink.

Bury your nose in a good book either on an electronic reader or on paper – whatever your pleasure. Dry airplane air and lack of sleep dries your eyes so treat your peepers to moisturizing drops as needed. As you finish books, leave them behind for other travelers to enjoy. It's good karma. Audio books are like hearing a childhood bedtime story. Try them and eyestrain will not be an issue.

Streamline Your Itinerary

Proper planning can reduce waiting. Planning your itinerary in advance will help get you those flights with the best connections. Get those admission tickets in advance to eliminate lines at popular tourist sites.

Pack Smart

With good packing practices, you will have what you need, when and where you need it. Your coat is packed in your carryon bag, and you are strolling the Champs-Élysées while your hotel room if your room is being prepared. Of course, you will feel better is you can refresh your face and brush your teeth upon arrival. Plan ahead and pack those important items for easy access.

AIRPORT WAITING

Treat Yourself

Channel your inner hedonist with a massage while you wait. Or grab that needed manicure or pedicure while you kill time at the airport.

If you are not a member of an airline club, consider a day pass to one. They provide a quiet oasis with many valuable amenities such as Internet service, drinks, snacks, comfortable seats, showers, and clean bathrooms with no lines.

Enjoy a good meal. Not all airport meals have to be overpriced sodium bombs. Many feature interesting options. Look for Vino Volo wine bars for some decent wine and a good casual entrée. In San Francisco you can get the real deal Irish Coffee from the iconic Buena Vista Café's airport location. Frankfurt, Germany is a generally unattractive and busy airport, but it is worth putting up with for a stop at Deutsch for a plate of sausage and sauerkraut.

Relax

Americans lead busy lives. We are all over-scheduled and stressed. We don't take time off. Try to view any time spent waiting as a gift of some downtime. People-watch. Stop. Breathe. Meditate. Think. It's all good.

ARRIVING

You've been sitting in the plane for how long? You've had plenty of time to calculate how long it has been since you woke up at home (and when you last showered). The best advice at this point in your journey is: GIVE IT UP. Put on your big-girl panties and move on. Do not dwell on how tired you are, how many time zones you have crossed, how long you've been traveling, or how horrible you smell.

Set your watch to the new time zone immediately. The best favor you can do for yourself is to promptly convert to local time for eating and sleeping. Embrace your new time zone.

Jet Lag – Curse of the Jet Set

If you are someone who handles jet lag well, my hat is off to you. You are lucky, indeed. It affects all of us, but some travelers absorb the ordeal of crossing multiple time zones with little impact, and others are debilitated.

The rule of thumb is that it takes your circadian rhythms one day to adjust for every time zone crossed. Flying from the West Coast to Abu Dhabi leaps 12 zones, hence you need 12 days to adjust, and this is true on both ends of your trip.

I find myself more motivated to push through it at the beginning of a trip, when there is so much I want to do and see. Whether my trip is from east to west or west to east, the return home is more difficult, probably due to the emotional letdown that comes at trip's end.

Jet lag manifests itself in both obvious and subtle ways. These can include **problems getting to and staying asleep, disorientation, headaches, dizziness, mood changes, irregularity, lack of coordination, inability to concentrate, swelling of limbs, and more.**

There are methods to employ before, during, and after travel to help ease or prevent some of the symptoms. No medication, herb, or plan eliminates jet lag completely, however. It's a real physiological condition with a medical name: *desynchronosis,* meaning out of sync with time.

Great travel tip: When suffering with jet lag, be careful crossing streets, especially where the traffic flow may be different than what you are accustomed to. Use care in performing activates requiring balance or when operating machinery, including a car.

If you arrive in daylight:

As tired as you may be, with as little sleep as you might have had en route, it's important to get into the sunlight and stay awake. Check the safety of the neighborhood and take a brisk walk. Exercise helps to restore circulation and wake you up. Sunlight aids in resetting your inner clock. It is important to use the light and darkness cycle to cue your body to be either awake or asleep.

If you arrive at night:

Go to sleep. Follow your usual bedtime rituals. Doing so helps your body recognize the cues for relaxation and sleep. Use a sleep aid, if needed. Wake up in the morning, ready to go.

Are you familiar with the 4-7-8 breathing technique, based on a yoga exercise espoused by Dr. Andrew Weil? The short explanation of it is that you inhale for a count of four, hold that breath for a count of seven, and exhale to a count of eight. This is to be repeated for four breath cycles. It is said to induce relaxation and sleep. Check it out.

Heed the local time and avoid napping. Naps trick your body into thinking that it's time to sleep during daylight. You'll fall sound asleep in the middle of the day, then not be able to sleep at night.

Does anybody really know what time it is?

In my younger life, converting time involved counting forward or backward on my fingers. Thankfully, those days are gone. You no longer need to know the Greenwich Mean Time plus or minus factor.

1. Your cell phone should be showing the correct local time.
2. Use the app on your phone to see any time in the world.
3. Your computer will do it for you. Google "time conversion," and you will find plenty of sites that perform the conversion for free.

Did you know the entire country of India is on the same time zone, and it is a half-hour off from the rest of the world? Smart thinking, India!

Great travel tip: If your travel is in spring or fall, be sure to know if and when your host country changes to or from Daylight Saving Time. Your hotel will probably let you know, but it may change your planning a bit, and it could cause you to miss your train!

Great travel tip: Set your cell phone timer for the flight time the pilot gives at the beginning of the flight. It is an easy way to know approximately how much longer until you get there. There also may be a map in the plane's entertainment system that shows the remaining time left in the flight.

How long does it take to get there?

This is the adult version of the child's question, "Are we there yet?"

Easiest: Look at your itinerary. Most computer-generated itineraries include the travel time.

Easier: Call the airline or travel agent and ask them. Their computers do it automatically.

SAVE YOUR TIME

There is a fine line between maximizing every minute of your trip and being over-scheduled to the point of ruining your enjoyment. One of the biggest challenges of any trip is that there is rarely enough time to accomplish everything you want.

Some of the best help you will get in this battle is from of a qualified travel agent who can streamline your itinerary and maximize your efficiency.

Give yourself permission to **allow for some flexibility or down time.** It can be used to see that exhibit you didn't know was in town or to linger in that charming Alpine village for a few more hours. You might need time to do laundry or simply wish to sleep in. I suggest you schedule an extra half-day about every fourth day. Float time really is OK, even when you travel!

Daylight is prime time to see sights. Use non-daylight hours to move. Taking night trains maximizes your daylight time for activity. You also save money by not paying for a hotel room when you sleep on the train.

Look for a nighttime city tour. You will pick up facts while enjoying the illumination of local monuments and buildings. Cities such as Washington D.C. and Paris are known for such tours. London offers a Jack the Ripper night tour and Savannah has an entertaining ghost tour.

Many museums offer one day a week with extended evening hours, thus leaving daytime hours free for other pursuits. The one museum where I suggest *not* going at night is the Musee d'Orsay in Paris. Its Impressionist art pieces benefit from the natural light in the unique setting of a re-purposed train station.

As mentioned previously, **museum passes** eliminate the need to wait in line for tickets. That adds up.

Some sights and museums accept reservations, and with some you must have a timed entry booked in advance or you will not be admitted. The Uffizi in Florence is a line you want to avoid, along with the one to see Michelangelo's David at the Accademia Gallery. Da Vinci's "Last Supper" in Milan is almost impossible to see without a reservation; only 25 people are admitted at a time. The Eiffel Tower lines are hours long, but with a timed admission purchased online, you enter at the appointed time, are whisked to the top and are back down well before you could have gotten through the waiting line to go up. From Disney Parks to the Vatican, a good travel agent will be able to get you on a fast track, skip the line, or early entry plan.

Compare rail tickets, driving, and flying for time and cost. When more than two people travel together, it may be less expensive to rent a car, but how much time will it take? How much stress is involved? Factor transfer times and costs to and from airports or train stations into your decision making process.

CHAPTER 10

Beauty on the Road

OK, WE'RE ALL GIRLS HERE, AND STAYING pretty is one of our big concerns. Being away from our own bathroom mirrors provides some challenges, but we can do this and do it well. Begin by giving yourself permission to relax your standards a bit. You are probably not competing in a beauty contest. Airplane headrests, sunhats, rain showers, and sweat are part of a traveler's reality. But guess what? Everyone else is in the same boat.

Let's separate toiletries such as shampoo and deodorant from makeup such as foundation and mascara for purposes of this discussion.

TOILETRIES IN THE BAG

Men must design hotel bathrooms. Otherwise, why do these bathrooms rarely have enough counter space for the items women bring? Meanwhile, they never seem large enough for two people to navigate them at the same time. Be prepared for the fact that space is tight and horizontal space is limited.

A toiletry **bag that can hang on the door hook** will help. Choose a bag with clear plastic pockets so you can see at a glance what's inside. Sometimes, because it fits better in my suitcase, I take a boxy-shaped toiletries bag that then has to sit on the floor or even on the toilet tank – this is a risky business and can lead to some unpleasant scenarios. Apply your makeup at the mirror in the sleeping area if there is good light there and you are sharing space. Both of you deserve some privacy in the bathroom area.

Separate like items. Keep together the things you use at the same time. You may end up with a bag for bedtime ritual items, one for hair-care, a different one for after showering, and one for things you use on your teeth. Separate first aid tools from daily medications.

When you get tired of constantly repacking your toiletry bag, just **keep one packed all the time.** My to-go bag duplicates what I use at home, plus a few emergency products. But each is in travel or sample size, or transferred to a small container from the larger one.

This is a situation I see time and again: Travelers pack full sized shampoo, makeup, and toothpaste in their luggage, adding unnecessary weight. Make sure you take the smallest amount required to lighten your load. I have squeezed the contents out of a travel-size toothpaste to see measure how long it would last. I order my deodorant online to get the smallest size available. Every ounce counts!

TOILETRIES CHECKLIST

- [ ] Shampoo and conditioner
- [ ] Deodorant
- [ ] Toothbrush, toothpaste, and floss
- [ ] Bandages
- [ ] Moleskin
- [ ] First aid items – see Chapter 14 for a list
- [ ] Hair products, gel, mousse, spray
- [ ] Hairbrush/comb
- [ ] Facial cleanser
- [ ] Toner
- [ ] Eye mask and earplugs
- [ ] Eye drops
- [ ] Lip balm
- [ ] Antibacterial soap
- [ ] Razor
- [ ] Shave cream
- [ ] Sunscreen
- [ ] Magnifying mirror
- [ ] Tweezers
- [ ] Medications

Other pointers:

- As your favorite blush, mascara, or other beauty products begin to run low at home, toss it in the travel bag and buy a new one. The small amount left is perfect for travel. When it runs out on the road, toss it!

- Be ready for your close-up with a **10x magnifying mirror**. It's my best brow-taming weapon in combo with my Tweezerman tweezers. I use one that's round and about 3.5 inches across, with suction cups on the back.

- **Antibacterial soaps** help prevent itching, heat rash, and discomfort and are especially useful in warm, humid climates.

MAKEUP

The first order of business: **Pare down.** For those who could fill their carry-on with their beauty products, a single compact of eyeshadows will do. Get your lashes and brows tinted or get lash extensions. Those will last several weeks and possibly eliminate the need for mascara and brow pencils. Can you get by with one lipstick? And again, move things into small containers.

By packing makeup in a separate pouch from toiletries, you've created a portable vanity that will go anywhere. Mine is in a 4"x6" bag. Here is a list for you to check:

- ☐ Moisturizer
- ☐ Foundation
- ☐ Blush
- ☐ Concealer
- ☐ Highlighter
- ☐ Mascara and eyelash curler

- ☐ Eye shadow
- ☐ Brow pencil
- ☐ Lip liner
- ☐ Lipstick
- ☐ Cosmetic brushes

YOU SMELL GOOD

Neither your signature $300 or $30 bottle of perfume belong on a trip. They're inclined to leak, and most do not comply with the TSA security rules covered in Chapter 7. My friend Sally offers this idea for taking your favorite fragrance: Spray a few applications into a small bottle of unscented body lotion. Shake it, and you have your fix.

GROOMING BEFORE YOU GO

Begin your trip with a fresh haircut and color, and a manicure and pedicure. Your time away is not well spent in a nail salon in Timbuktu, although that would be an adventure.

Have nails cut short enough to survive your trip. A good application of polish will protect them from the travails of travel. I've become a convert to shellac polish, which lasts up to three weeks if I use a light neutral color that minimizes the demarcation of grow out.

Extend the life of your traditional manicure by reapplying the topcoat every couple of days. Seal the topcoat bottle in a Ziploc bag or a plastic pill bottle to protect it from breaking. If you can, take a bottle that's almost empty. The Go Girls motto: Less is more.

Pack a nail file and nail clippers if you use them. Clippers can go in your carry-on bag if they don't have a blade. Avoid a metal or glass file if you are flying. If you find a rough spot on a nail and are caught without a file, use the striking part of a matchbook to smooth it out.

HAIR TIPS

The rigors of travel present plenty of hair challenges. Hard water, soft water, no water, and no hot water – oh my! Transporting hair products and appliances compounds the issues. How do you avoid a bad-hair day?

You can't do much about the quality or availability of water. If your travel plans include locations without water to wash your hair, take a **dry shampoo.** There are several options; try one at home to see exactly how it works with your hair. Or plan on covering up with a hat or scarf.

Hair products and appliances are awkward and heavy. If you're traveling abroad, you'll have to deal with the associated problems of electric voltage, converters, and adapters. If you can, leave them at home. Most hotels have hair dryers in the rooms or available at the front desk. In place of curling and straightening appliances, **experiment with Velcro rollers or a butane curling or flat iron.** A mother and daughter who regularly travel with me approach their curly locks in two different ways: Mom embraces her curls, and daughter dons a ponytail. With my fine, straight hair, I am envious of both.

Create ways to capture a look with the least effort. Add an ornament: headband, scarf, clips, bow, live or silk flowers, rhinestones, ribbons, and faux tortoise shell. These also can help you make an effective transition from day to evening. The same black sweater and pants goes effectively from day to evening with only a simple change of hair accessories.

Great travel tip: **Be extremely cautious about having your nails done while traveling abroad. An infection or fungus is not the exotic souvenir you are looking to bring home.**

Fake hair is a lifesaver. Yes, fake hair! On a Danube River cruise, I spent the day touring in the pouring rain. Upon return to my stateroom, I found slipped under my cabin door an invitation to dine with the captain in a half-hour. I showered, dashed on makeup and clothes, and pulled my fairly short hair into a pathetic ponytail. Over it I clipped a hairpiece, gave it a good spray and then headed out the door to the captain's table. Voila!

CHAPTER 11

Enjoying Your Trip

You've ARRIVED AT YOUR DESTINATION. The good time you've been waiting for is there at your feet. All those well-wishes from friends are ringing in your ears. Have a great time, they all said. Now let's take it from good to great with these tips.

THE FINEST THINGS IN LIFE

Buying Art

Purchasing art is a wonderful way to bring home a piece of another culture. Original art is duty-free, so it can be a bargain. But how do you get it home?

For posters and paintings, **take a mailing tube.** Nest one in the bottom edge of your luggage. Stuff it with lingerie, socks or an umbrella. Roll the art and carry it in the tube. Depending on its fragility and value, you can either put it back into your bag or hand-carry it. Yes, you can look all over Beijing for an open stationery store in order to buy a mailing tube, instead. This is the easy way.

I am not an art critic but this much I can tell you: **Buy what**

you like and can afford. Generally, art purchased by tourists is unlikely to work as an investment. Rather, it is something you can enjoy in your home and share with guests while fondly remembering the place and events that surrounded its purchase.

Shaken Not Stirred

A full flask is a friend you may want to have. Flasks aren't just for college boys; they come dressed in pink alligator and leopard prints for the fairer sex, too. Just remember when it is full to pack it in a checked bag, not a carry-on. You are not encouraged to bring your own alcohol on the plane, even if it is under 3 ounces!

Not dressed for the hotel bar but feeling like a cocktail while preparing for your night out? Don't want to sit at the bar alone? Traveling where distilled spirits are very expensive? Bring out the flask to save some money, and maybe some frustration.

My drink of choice is the vodka martini, a simple concoction that can still come out wrong. In India my order came with a black olive in sweet pink vermouth. Cruising along the Nile River, I didn't know why the drink was so bad until I received the bill: I'd been charged for two drinks, vodka and vermouth. They had been mixed together in equal parts. Yuck!

My secret weapon is to **pre-mix my drink** at home. Add the vodka and vermouth into the flask and screw on the lid. If I can't find a lemon twist or olive at my destination, I can live without it. An easy Manhattan can be put together with your favorite recipe too. Or fill your flask with straight liquor and find a mixer on the road. No refrigeration necessary. Just add ice. Cheers!

If you drink decaf coffee or herbal tea, you might need to pack your own. Decaf usually translates as Sanka or Nescafe. If you need a more upscale version, buy Starbuck's Via packets. Although herbal teas can be hard to find in some locations, your travels may introduce you to new varieties that tempt your palate. I was introduced to Rooibos on a British ship in Antarctica and masala chai in India. I enjoy having chamomile tea on long flights to help me sleep. The flight attendant brings me hot water, and I make my own. It is also a nice way to unwind before bed after a hectic day.

The Swiss Army Rides to the Rescue

My trusty Swiss Army knife makes me feel like a traveling MacGyver. Its important functions include cutting cheese and opening wine bottles. Regulations make it difficult to take along; it cannot be in a carry-on bag. If you travel with only a carry-on, you can purchase a pocketknife and/or corkscrew at your destination. Mine has treated me to uncounted gourmet picnics, extracted too many eyebrow hairs to mention, and snipped many a loose thread.

WINERIES AND DISTILLERIES

Some of my favorite travel adventures have focused on visiting wineries and distilleries around the world. The You Go Tastefully part of my company conducts tours to them. I have seen production of rum, scotch, tequila, cognac, grappa, bourbon, and whiskey. Because my husband and I own a vineyard, I've worked in the tasting rooms of neighbors and friends.

Regarding a winery visit: If the winery has a public tasting room, it should have posted operating hours. Honor them. In many small operations, the winemakers live on-site, and you will inconvenience them if you visit outside posted hours.

If you inadvertently arrive outside business hours and the winemaker offers a tour and/or tasting, accept his or her hospitality, but plan on purchasing some wine to show your appreciation. If the winery is not generally open to the public or you need to make an appointment, give adequate notice and be patient when you arrive. The proprietors could be in the south forty or blending in the lab!

Tasting fees aren't always communicated well. **Ask questions freely** regarding costs, processes, or products. It is the staff's job to welcome and educate you so that you will purchase their products. If you are a novice, say so. You will be instructed about how to see, swirl, sniff, sip, spit or swallow, and savor.

Wineries and distilleries provide tastings to make money. If they are giving you a free tasting, their remuneration is your purchase. Sometimes if there is a tasting fee it is credited toward a purchase. Some tasting room staff will accept gratuities, you can leave a tip when you feel that you've been given special treatment.

Avoid wearing perfume or any scented products when touring or tasting. One of the most critical components of taste is smell. Your Shalimar is not a desirable characteristic of chardonnay for either you or those who may smell it. **Chewing gum ruins your sense of taste. Never smoke near people who are tasting.** High alcohol levels in production facilities also make it dangerous to smoke.

At a serious tasting, allow everyone to taste before voicing your impressions. Your suggestion may affect other drinkers' impressions.

The food offered in a tasting room is not to be considered as a meal, but rather as a chance to cleanse the palate or enhance the enjoyment of the wine. So, when going out for a serious day of tasting, **take your own food pairing kit.** It could include cheeses, nuts, some sausages, and chocolate to pair with the wine. A bottle of water and bland crackers will give your palate a break. Your bandana will come in handy to wipe out your glass between wineries.

A **Tide To Go or Wine Away spray is a great addition** to your kit in the event of a red wine splash. Avoid wearing white or your Sunday best. Many wineries offer their own clean glasses, but on busy event weekends you may be required to purchase a glass or provide your own.

It is **not necessary to rinse your glass** with water between tastes. The tastes are small, and you would end up with watery wine and the next wine will not properly show its properties. As you proceed from light to heavier wines, you'll go from whites to reds. You would rinse your glass if, for some reason, you were going from a red back to a white in order to not compromise the color. Just a tiny bit of red wine will turn a white to pink. Rinsing with wine is offered in some places and is a good practice.

It is **OK to use the dump bucket.** On the tasting table there should be a container to dispose of wine. Perhaps you do not like the wine after giving it two tastes, or maybe you are trying to limit the amount you are drinking. Whatever the reason, do not feel badly about pouring out your wine. Not all of us like the same things, if we did, there would not be enough of it.

The process for distillery tastings is much the same as for a wine tasting. However, with distilled spirits, the alcohol levels are higher. Be very careful.

Enjoy the experience, assign a designated driver, and consume responsibly. Many countries have a zero-tolerance for drinking and driving. We do not want to be sending your mail to the Chateauneuf-du-Pape jail!

Taking It Home

Wine needs to be kept from extreme temperature fluctuations. A

Great travel tip: When possible, purchase more than one bottle of the wine you choose. You will want one to try at home, one to share with friends, and probably – another to have again later at home. Trust me on this.

car that is too hot for the dog is too hot for your wine. An insulated cooler will help keep the temperature even.

If you are bringing home a case, the people at Wine Check (thewinecheck.com) have developed a great product for flyers. Their bag, when filled with 12 wine bottles, will be under the current airline weight limit for a single bag. It is on wheels, so it's easy to move. You will be charged the checked bag fee, but that may be less expensive than shipping a case home.

Some winemaking areas have forged agreements with airlines, allowing you to check a box of wine at no charge. That includes your Wine Check bag.

It is hard on wine to fly. It goes into bottle shock from the shaking of travel. Give it a couple of days to settle down again. Flights can also expose it to extreme temperature variation. Most wineries will not ship wine during certain months of the year for that reason. Enjoy sharing your treats with friends at home. Cheers!

SPAS

Whether dropping in to the hotel spa for a quick mani or spending a week at a destination spa, the protocols are the same.

- **Make appointments in advance.** There is no guarantee of service for drop-ins. Once you have made your appointment, you must **be on time.** If you are late, your appointment may be shortened.

- **Be clear on cancellation policies.** Most service providers will charge for a missed appointment.

- **Arrive early enough to complete paperwork,** especially on your first visit.

- **Come clean or showered**. Would you want to perform a pedicure on dirty feet or massage a sweaty body?

- **Turn off your cell phone.** This is time for relaxation. Everyone is paying good money for this pleasure. Your phone conversation is not relaxing for others who can hear it.

- **Ask about amenities in advance.** Do they have robes, slippers, a steam room, or a relaxation room? Ask if there is a shower facility for using before or after your service. After your massage, you may want to shower off the oil or lotion.

- **Tip 15 to 20 percent.** Tips can be left in the treatment room, given at the point of payment, or handed directly to the therapist. Some places offer an envelope in which to place your tip, and usually the preferred method of payment is cash. Ask about the policy to be clear.

- **Use a quiet spa voice for conversations.** Sound travels, and sometimes there is little separating service areas. If the therapist talks more than you wish, there is nothing wrong with saying, "I am going to enjoy my quiet time now. Let's chat later."

Rub Me the Right Way

Treating yourself to a massage away from home is a wonderful way to unwind, relax, and experience special regional delights such as grape seed scrubs, Thai massage, Dead Sea mud masks, and tropical aromatherapy.

After a long camel ride, miles of shopping, or a day of bus riding driven on the LEFT side of the road, there's nothing like a massage. Having indulged in this decadent pleasure all over the world, I can vouch for its power.

As with most new experiences in strange places, communication is key. The therapist WANTS to know if you are comfortable but she or he does not have ESP. Just ask for more or less pressure and remember that a massage should feel good and not induce pain. Speak up if you want to change the temperature in the room or if the heated towels or hot packs are not comfortable. This is YOUR massage and it should be all you desire.

Getting naked for a massage is not comfortable for everyone. You will receive a more effective massage if the therapist doesn't have to work around clothing, but **your comfort trumps all else.** Feel free request your preference for a male or female therapist. And do remove all jewelry. It is very difficult to work around and it can cause pain.

Great travel tip: For a Thai massage they supply a pajama-like cotton outfit for you to wear. You are not naked.

HOME AWAY FROM HOME

Your hotel room is your sanctuary. Whether you are a business traveler making sales calls and conducting meetings all day, or a tourist dealing with crowds, street vendors, and the vagaries of weather, you want to personalize that room into your own private refuge.

One of the first ways to do this is **to deal with the bedspread.** Spreads are not laundered after each guest. Think about the last person who drooled on that bedspread. No, don't! Take it off, fold it down, or at least, fold a sheet over the top edge of it.

Next, bring in **fresh flowers.** They feed your eyes, nose, and soul. A soda can or wine bottle will work as a vase. Even a single dandelion offers a dash of color to make you smile.

Light a nice candle if your room smells stuffy or stale. I carry a rose-scented one with a lid that's sold as a travel candle. Not only does it smell good, it casts a pretty light. Be responsible. Do not burn it while you sleep or are out of the room.

An alternative is a room spray or plug-in room fresheners (carry only in a checked bag if it contains more than your 3 ounces of liquid). I have discovered **Scentsy** products. They offer a multitude of fragrances, none of which requires a burning wick. Among their travel-friendly items is one that works like a sachet and is great for keeping luggage fresh. Their product called Odor Out counteracts malodors. The company offer products in more than 80 fragrances. Independent consultants sell them (I am not one). You can find them on the Internet.

Yankee Candle has a range of nice products to mask odors and give you a dose of pleasure in your home away from home. They come in beautiful scents, colors, and forms.

Ask for a change if your room is too bright or too noisy. If pulling the curtains still leaves it too bright, use your eye mask and seal up any curtain gap with a bit of duct tape, a clothespin, or paper clip.

Earplugs may save light sleepers from the unfamiliar hotel noises or overly amorous neighbors. You should still be able to hear the alarm and the phone. You can also request a quiet room when

Great travel tip: Check the alarm settings on the bedside clock before you retire. It could be still set for the people who checked out before you and booked the sunrise volcano tour the day before.

making your reservation. That will likely mean you give up a quaint street view at the front on the hotel, but a good night's sleep may be well worth it.

EAT LOCAL, DRINK LOCAL

Enjoying local cuisine accomplishes more than adding to your waistline. It exposes you to local ingredients and gives insight into a culture. To say food grounds us is more than a clever pun. **Food connects us to the earth. It also connects us to people.** The cheese in the fondue comes from the cows, goats, or sheep chomping grass on that hillside. Sharing the pot of fondue around the table puts us shoulder to shoulder with people and their lives. Conversations ensue, and suddenly we are immersed in one of those travel experiences forever etched in our memories.

And while you're eating native, go ahead and **drink native**, too. The pinot noirs of the Willamette Valley are a perfect match to the salmon caught in the very river that runs through it. Wiener schnitzel pairs beautifully with the Austrian Gruner Veltliner. Food and wine that come from the same *terrior*, the same soil and environment, go together like a horse and carriage. Go ahead and try the Hungarian goulash, Roquefort, Greek olives, and Spanish almonds. Drink the Tokay, Riesling, retsina, pilsner, slivovitz, and calvados. And, for those inclined to the exotic, reindeer meat and sea urchins await you!

OH, MY ACHING FEET

A full day of sightseeing takes a toll on feet. Bring along a small amount of massage lotion to treat your feet. Mint oil, cinnamon, sage, Epsom salts, and ice can offer relief too.

Pack a tennis ball for a very effective foot massage.
Rolling your foot over it improves circulation and gives sore
foot muscles a good stretch. It works well on the back, too.
Place it between your back and the back of a chair for some
pressure-point work.

If you are traveling in Asia, it is easy to find a professional
foot massage at a great price. In other areas it will be more
expensive but may still be worth the splurge. Just say, ahhh.

PEOPLE TO PEOPLE

Now that you're immersed in your destination, you are bound
to encounter children. Giving gifts to children brings up
a plethora of issues. As women, we are often drawn to children, and when we find them living in what we perceive are
unhealthy conditions, we feel compelled to help them. At one
point in my travel life, I thought that good quality or healthy
gifts were a positive way to make connections with them. I gave
pens, erasers, notebooks, and toothbrushes as alternatives to the
candy and gum given by many tourists.

As I have seen more of the world, I have changed my out-
look. All gifts have impacts you may not have considered. I
have seen near riots break out, with children knocking each
other to the ground in order to get a gift. I have witnessed
them using devious methods to score multiple gifts. The
impact of one child in a village or a family showing up with
a gift when the others didn't have the opportunity to receive
one can be devastating to a little person's psyche. Furthermore, it encourages kids to expect gifts and to beg for them,
sometimes at the expense of spending time in school.

Purchasing items from children who should be in school

A foot soak can be the
perfect recipe for relax-
ation. This is the DIY
one that I use. Choose
your favorite scent to
enhance your sensory
enjoyment.

Fantastic Foot Soak
¼ cup Epsom salts
¼ cup sea salt
¼ cup baking soda
A few drops of your
favorite essential oil to
suit your mood.
Lavender, lemongrass,
eucalyptus and vanilla
are great options.

Directions:

Mix dry ingredients in a
glass bowl. Add the oil of
your choice and mix until
blended. Seal in con-
tainer for travel.

Add 2 tablespoons to a
basin of water. Adjust
the water temperature
to your preference.

Great travel tip:
Please do not give children sugary treats. They may not even have access to a toothbrush. You are not doing them a favor.

also discourages them from getting an education. At the same time, their sales also may be providing an important income to a family. Do you see how complex it becomes?

If you want to change the world by helping children, donate to a well-managed and responsible charity. You will feel the satisfaction of helping and you will have accomplished it in a constructive way. Please examine such charities such as Mercy Corps, Samaritan's Purse, and World Vision. With a small amount of research, you will find an organization that uses your donation to accomplish some real good.

Hostess gifts offer a different challenge. Consider how complex gift-giving is within your own family. Expand that to a different culture, and it becomes mind-boggling. Conde Nast offers a starting point with this excellent article: cntraveler.com/stories/2011-03-15/etiquette-101-what-gives.

Years ago, I was the guest of a lovely business acquaintance in Bangkok. The dramatic orchid sprays sold by the hotel florist seemed a perfect hostess gift. When I asked my guide for a suggestion, he suggested I give her a *maneki-neko*, the "fortune cat," one of those statuettes of a cat with the raised paw. I was appalled, regarding the statue as a kitschy souvenir. I met my hostess at the appropriate time, my orchids in hand. We were shown to our seats, and as I looked around, I realized that the place was full of orchids. In Thailand, orchids are nothing special. The "fortune cat," thought to summon money and success in that country, would have, indeed, been the better choice given our business relationship.

An alternative to divining what is an appropriate hostess gift in another culture is to bring unique items from home, such as picture books, local packaged foods, or crafts.

Postcards from your hometown are fun to share with new friends. A map of the world, your country and your state help others to put you and your home into geographic perspective. I have even packed an inflatable globe to share with children. **Photos of your family** are also nice to show. Be careful about showing pictures of your house and car. It's not only insensitive with people who live in more humble circumstances than you do, but it may put you in a situation for people to want to take advantage of you.

Items that can be shared build special moments together. You are not going to give these away. Games to play together, songs, and magic tricks fall into this category. Shared smiles go a long way toward world understanding. Use them freely and frequently.

CHAPTER 12

Ways to Travel

$\mathcal{Say}$ THE WORD "TRAVEL." FOR SOME OF US, it is synonymous with "vacation." For others, however, it's to earn or to learn. While types of travel may differ, so too may our travel companions. Traveling in a group or with children requires a special set of skills.

NOT STRICTLY BUSINESS

Business travelers, you can also inject some fun into your time away. Try to fit in a tour or an activity in a new city. If you make frequent visits to the same places, join a local club or museum, or set a goal to try a new restaurant each time you are there. A friend whose work took him to Dubai many times broadened his perspective of what was previously just his workplace by visiting a cultural center on one visit.

Inviting a friend along can turn an otherwise boring business trip into a mini-vacation. Can you extend your trip to take advantage of the weekend and see the area?

The bonus of business travel is that most employers allow you to keep your frequent flyer membership miles for personal use. Each business trip gets you that much closer to a free vacation flight.

PRIVATE RENTALS

The rental of private homes and apartments is a fast growing and popular source of accommodations for travelers. You know them by names such as AirBnB and VRBO (Vacation Rental by Owner). Home exchanges and villa rentals also fall into this category.

The host makes money providing a property for rental. You get rich cultural and personal experiences. There is no room service, no cheery concierge at your beck and call, no sumptuous spa, or lavish breakfast. The benefits are in rubbing shoulders with real people and learning to live as they do. Walking through the neighborhood, shopping in the market, using local transportation and sharing a meal in the corner pub give an unmatched perspective.

As you search, book, and use these types of accommodations, there are different considerations and concerns to take into account. You are working without a net, so be smart.

Private-party rentals versus rental companies

Booking with private individuals is full of unknowns. Great and special cautions should be taken with any rentals from strangers. You have heard the exposés of people showing up to a private rental and finding it occupied or never existed. There are stories of squatters offering rental properties that do not belong to them.

You are not going to have backup. You will be on your own to contact the owner to deal with the ants in the kitchen or the leak in the bathroom. These can work out well, especially if you know someone else who can attest to the quality of the rental. Be wary and enter with caution.

Use a reputable company

A reputable rental company is a key to success. Use one with a history of successful service. They should be willing to share their guidelines as to how they process your payments, the inspection and rating of their properties, and provide information regarding the level at which their hosts and guests are vetted. In some situations, you may not only be sharing space with the host but with other renters. This might include sharing a bathroom. It is a leap of faith to trust that everything will go smoothly and be within your comfort zone.

Know what you are getting into

Women traveling alone should pay attention to the safety of different scenarios. If you are sharing space with others, you want assurances that you will be safe. Pay particular attention to the safety of the neighborhood since you will be spending time in it and traveling in and out of it.

Rentals include a wide range of options including simple room rentals with a shared bath and/or kitchen, city apartments, farmhouses, resorts, and villas. In some cases, personable owners are present, sharing space or adjacent spaces. In others, you may have no contact. You will be given instructions for independent check-in and check-out.

Each arrangement suits different personalities and serves a range of needs. A villa for 20 people for a culinary group gives each couple a private room and a shared swimming pool. The large kitchen allows for cooking classes and group preparation. A single room in a large house with multiple rooms can be just the right way for a single woman to feel safe and connected when traveling alone. A couple may enjoy a small urban apartment as a base from which to explore. Evaluate your tolerance for privacy, quiet, cleanliness, safety, and cost before you commit.

Communications

A good rental company should have efficient methods of communication between renters and hosts to answer questions and meet expectations. These questions provide the starting points.

QUESTIONS TO ASK

What deposits are required?
    How are they paid?
    Are they refundable?

When is the balance due?
    How is it paid?

What is the check-in and check-out policy?

What beds are in each room and how large are they?

How many bathrooms are there and where are they located?

What supplies are included as part of the rental - bed and bath linens, basic condiments, soap, paper goods?

Are there cleaning supplies?

Is cleaning service provided during your stay?

Are there surcharges for heating, cooling, utilities, etc.? These are encountered more than you may think. In some places, heating and cooling may function before or after a certain calendar date.

Is there reliable Internet service and/or phone service for free or for a cost?

Do the facilities meet your cooking needs?
>Are you cooking large meals for a group or just coffee for 2?
>Is breakfast provided?
>Is there a cook or can one be hired?
>>Does the cost for a cook include food costs or just service?

What are the laundry facilities? Some places it is customary to have a washer but not a dryer.
>Is there a fee?
>Is detergent supplied?

What about other appliances?
>How large is the refrigerator?
>Is the stove gas or electric?
>Is there a microwave?
>Is there a coffee maker?

Is there grocery shopping nearby?
>Will you need transportation to get to a market?
>What are its hours and days of operation? Take your own grocery bags. Most places do not supple them.

PACKING FOR RENTING

Once your questions are answered, it is time to plan and pack.
>If you are in need of small amounts of **condiments**, this is a

time when www.minimus.biz can help. Small ketchup, mustard, hot sauce, mayonnaise, and spices are a part of their inventory. Pack your own if you anticipate they may be hard to find. In my many visits to Mexico, whipping up an Indian curry recipe seemed like the perfect use for the wonderful freshly caught shrimp. We searched the supermarket for curry powder. Try explaining that in Spanish to a grocery worker. After many trials at pantomiming, we ultimately found it not to exist and took to taking our own for future visits.

If you are planning to do serious cooking – take your own **knives**. A chef's knife and paring knife are the two most basic. Think ahead and take what you need. Knives are the most misused and abused piece of kitchen equipment in rentals. They are often dangerously dull and frustrating to use if you have any expectation of proper food preparation.

Are there certain **items you are just cannot live without**? If you absolutely must have drip coffee in the morning then you need to know if there is a proper coffee maker. In Australia and other tea drinking countries, many kitchens only have an electric kettle and instant coffee. Others may have a French press or a single serving brewer.

Use a **delivery service** to have groceries ready for your arrival. The owner or rental company may offer one, or you can find your own. Have you thought about having a **meal service delivered** so you have what you need to make a nice meal? Think Blue Apron and Hello Fresh within the U.S.

Pack any cleaning supplies you have strong feeling about. As an example, if you love sponges and not dishrags, take your own or be prepared to shop.

HEED THE REVIEWS

The comments of previous guests are their gift to you. Comb

through them. Reading between the lines of those reviews will lead you to very important facts that may not be clearly stated in the host's description.

Reports of noise levels, cleanliness, directions to the property, and supplies will assist in your knowledge of what to expect. Those restaurant recommendations and suggestions for side trips, guides, and drivers, are like gold.

These reviews are the best independent information you can get. Read the good ones and the bad ones. Consider who wrote them. People from different countries have different expectations. Try to discern if negative issues presented are a function of personalities or actual conditions and situations.

BE A GOOD GUEST

You may be asked for feedback on your rental and the host can also rate you as a guest. Poor communication is the cause of most misunderstandings between renter and host. Do your part by follow the guidelines set by the host and you should garner a positive review for yourself. Comply with house rules regarding check in and out procedures, partying, noise, security, handling of garbage, and clean up. Leave the property in the condition you found it.

Give positive feedback in a timely manner and carefully approach negative issues without personal attacks. Negative feedback can help improve future rentals for others if presented in a kind and helpful manner sandwiched with a compliment. As an example - when painting is going on in the building, remark that it will certainly be nice when it is completed but the odor was bothersome during the rental period and was not warned of. You will catch more flies with honey than with vinegar.

Consider the reviews that were helpful to you and write ones that will help others who come after you.

If this fits your travel style, take advantage and be exposed to some unforgettable experiences.

THE TRAVELING OFFICE

A retired flight attendant taught me how to take the office with me wherever I go. I carry a small pouch containing a few **paper clips, rubber bands, and folded blank envelopes** – all versatile items that can be used in multiple ways. The envelopes can deliver a message or a tip or organize receipts or documents. Paper clips can serve as little tools on the road. Toss in a **generic birthday card or blank card**. I add a **highlighter pen** and **Post-It notes** arrows, both useful for marking up travel books.

A **black or blue ballpoint point pen** is essential for filling out immigration forms. But seal pens; they can leak as a result of the change in pressure on the plane. A pen with colored ink can make your notes stand out. And I can't leave home without the humble pencil – **a mechanical pencil,** that is, with plenty of lead. If you like Sudokus and crossword puzzles, a wooden pencil will get dull, and the lead breaks. No sharpener needed with the mechanical version. Clip to to your notebook or puzzle in progress.

Speaking of puzzles, I cut them out of my newspaper on days when I don't have time to do them at home. I save them in a file to take when I travel. My client, Jan, carries a small clipboard that gives her a solid backing for solving puzzles any time, anywhere.

OFFICE PACKING LIST

- [ ] Business cards
- [ ] Black or blue ball point pen
- [ ] Colored ink pen
- [ ] Paper clip
- [ ] Mechanical pencil
- [ ] Highlighter pen
- [ ] Powerstrip/surge protector
- [ ] Post-It notes
- [ ] Rubber band
- [ ] Generic greeting card
- [ ] Envelopes
- [ ] Memory stick

A **power strip with surge protection** is a must if you have electronics to protect. You'll be the most popular person around if you share it with others in a crowded airport or meeting.

Even if you are not connected to a business, **business cards** can be a useful tool. They are easy to print with your computer and even easier to order professionally made. It is a convenient way to share your contact information when you travel. Do be careful about what personal information you share with strangers: Consider using a post office box rather than your home address, or set up a free email account solely for this purpose. You can always handwrite information as needed.

THE BUS TOUR

That tote bag can be your best friend for this mode of travel. It will **keep your belongings together and close by**. Fill it with extra shoes, a book, snacks to share, your camera, etc. Most bus drivers stay with the vehicle and will let you leave unneeded items on the bus. If you are going into a museum and are not allowed a camera, leave it on the bus in your tote. **Check the overhead storage, seat pocket and around your seat when you disembark at the end of the tour to collect all your items.**

To avoid frustration, before you book a tour, ask how many passengers they book per departure. Larger tours are less expensive but require more patience because of the number who must get on and off the bus at each stop. Weigh your options and your patience level.

On multi-day tours, your escort will probably have a protocol for switching seats. Go with the flow. You do not get to score a window seat each and every day. This is another question to ask. How many seats are on the bus compared to how many travelers?

If you are prone to motion sickness, let the guide know. You cannot be guaranteed a seat in the front of the bus. But you can try if that helps you. Be prepared with remedies such as ginger, **Dramamine,** or the acupressure based **Sea-Bands** as an alternative to drugs.

It is almost always appropriate to **tip your escort, guide, and driver.** Ask the tour company or travel agent for specific guidelines.

In the Running for Miss Popularity

Be on time or early for everything. It is as important to be on time for the beginning of activities as it is to return to the group on time as activities are completed.

Know the number of your bus and where and when you are to meet it. Write down the information on paper or commit it to your cell phone note page. Set an alarm on your phone if that helps. Tattoo it on your forehead if you must.

Be prepared and able to handle your own luggage, equipment, purchases, and accessories. Everyone has personal items to supervise, and women especially need to be accountable for their own belongings. Do not rely on a stranger or friend to help you.

Be prepared to **pay for meals, admissions, tips, and other similar charges with cash.** Separate checks are not always an option. When sharing the bill, it's extremely difficult to manage the math of multiple credit cards.

Hold the perfume. Fragrances in close quarters can play havoc with allergies and be unpleasant for those sensitive to smells. Adding cologne or perfume to everyday hair products, lotions, and fabric treatments can be overwhelming.

Develop **a plan for paying for meals, admissions, tips, etc.** Does everyone deposit money in a pool? Does each person handle individual costs, or do you divide costs evenly? Some but not all may order appetizers, desserts, or beverages in addition to the meal. There may be differing views on how much to tip. I cannot emphasize enough how important it is for EVERYONE to be in agreement on these systems. Arrive at a mutually agreeable solution in advance.

Your behavior reflects on the group. Loud talking, bad behavior, or ignorance of local sensitivities reflects on the whole group. So does your appearance.

CITY TOURS

Even the most independent travelers can benefit from a quick tour in a new city. Because of the nature of my work as a tour escort, I often have repeated city tours, and I learn something new each time. A guided tour efficiently gives you basic background and hangs your visit on the time frame of history. It becomes the starting point for developing a list of things you may want to independently explore later.

Audio tours are available for downloading so that you can walk a tour route on your own, but **nothing replaces the personal interaction from a certified local guide.** A good guide will have knowledge and the ability to share it using clear English. Increase your chances of getting a good one by using an established tour company.

Many companies now use headsets to amplify the guide's voice in a noisy city environment. However, if someone engages the guide in a side conversation, you can only hear the guide's response, which is frustrating.

Some countries have a guide certification program. In England they are Blue Badges. French and Italian guides are strictly regulated, too. Your travel agent is a good resource and can arrange tours in advance, with the added advantage that the cost is taken care of before you go. Or you can search sites such as viator.com, a tour broker, if you want to do it yourself. The companies Viator represents are generally reputable and very good.

If you have hearing issues or special needs, let the guide know before the tour begins so that you can be seated or positioned to optimize your understanding. Mentioning special needs when you book a tour will avoid disappointment. Mobility issues can often be accommodated with adequate warning. Elevators and wheelchairs may be available in many places. Some locations and excursions simply cannot accommodate anyone who is less than able because of fixed conditions such as elevation changes, stairs, uneven surfaces, or lack of handrails. If you cannot meet the requirements, don't put yourself or others at risk.

SHARING A ROOM

Respect, communication, and compromise are the keys to harmony. Because You Go Girls! Travel deals with groups, this is especially important to me, and those who travel with me.

Sleeping and waking are big concerns. How do early birds and night owls coexist? **Earplugs, eye masks, and courtesy** that's how. Reading in bed is easily accomplished with a flashlight or book light for the reader if the sleeper has an eye mask. If you need to make phone calls while your roommate sleeps, use the lobby.

As a courtesy, keep your roommate informed as to your whereabouts. **A phone call, note, or message is sufficient.** Decide in advance how you will communicate such information.

The hotel room is a haven for both guests. **It is not OK to entertain friends** of the same or opposite sex in the room without mutual agreement. This is a matter of safety as well as consideration. Don't put yourself, your roommate and your personal items at risk.

Borrowing items from a roommate without permission is strictly *verboten*. Enough said!

Sharing certain items can be a way to lighten your load, however. One iron, one hairdryer (if not provided in the room), and one electric converter could be enough for two. You could also share emergency first aid supplies. Communicate in advance.

Great travel tip: Whether for business or pleasure, consider arriving at your destination a day early. Treat yourself to a massage or a good meal in that downtime. You'll be that much more rested and ready to go when everyone else arrives.

The biggest issue for women who share a hotel room is deciding how to divvy up bathroom time. Two princesses may find this especially difficult! Try alternating between who showers first. If you need 30 minutes of uninterrupted bathroom time every morning after breakfast, you need to negotiate to get it. Remember there is usually a public bathroom someplace else in the hotel when schedules collide.

Keep your personal items on your designated side of the sleeping area and bathroom. If you are modest about undressing in front of your roommate, say so and set your boundaries at the start. As my therapist daughter-in-law would say, you are entitled to your feelings.

TRAVELING WITH KIDS

We are all women here. Many of us are grandmothers, mothers, aunts, older sisters, and a travel companion to a child at some time. Personally I have traveled with my own children and grandchildren. My multigenerational trips each year are well recieved. Grandmothers, moms, and aunts bring children along for international and domestic tours. I can speak to what works.

Traveling with a child is just that – traveling WITH a child. It is not your trip. It is not their trip. **It is your trip together.** WITH is the operative word here. Some adults are better than others at going with the flow and the same holds true for kids. We all bring different personalities and needs to the table.

Work toward a positive experience for yourself and the young person by paying special attention to these key points. Adjust them for age, theirs and yours!

- **Be patient.** Make a pact for everyone to be patient. Remind yourself and each other of the pact if things begin to slip. Losing your cool with a child can scare them, make them distrustful, and hurt their heart in a way you may not be able to fix.

- **Be prepared.** Travel can be unpredictable. Beat the system with snacks, toys or entertainment, a change of clothes, and any creature comfort you deem necessary. You never know when plans will change. I have been on two flights recently where adults vomited. That clean tee shirt could come in handy.

- **Be adaptable.** The weather changes and suddenly a day at the water park becomes a day at the museum. Teach your young one the ability to adapt. It is a skill that serves well through life. We taught our "littles" that sometimes Plan A becomes Plan B and on a bad day sometimes we get all the way to XYZ. Sometimes the alternative is better than the original plan. Make lemonade out of those lemons and set up a stand.

- **Be fed.** A hungry traveler is a grouchy traveler. This holds true for all ages. Healthy snacks can save the day. Carry them or stop for them.

- **Be rested.** If you think a hungry traveler is grouchy, look at a tired one. Meltdowns are on the horizon. Plan for downtime. Leave Disneyland and go back to the hotel for a swim and a rest. Then return to the park later in the day.

- **Be comfortable.** It is not fun to have squirming toddler on your lap for 9 hours. It is worse if they are screaming. Talk with your doctor about how to relieve the ear pain that many small children get when flying. Their ears do not adjust to the pressurization of the plane and it is excruciatingly painful. There are simple solutions.

- **Get the wiggles out.** Kids need to blow off steam. A visit to Central Park, Luxembourg Gardens, or Hyde Park is enjoyable for you while providing an opportunity for needed exercise.

- **Plan appropriate activities.** Children and adults may be attracted to different activities. Do things that interest them and you, but mostly them, for a positive experience. Zoos, parks, museums with hands-on exploration, and various forms of transportation are some ideas. Each child is different as is each adult. Some have more tolerance than others for museums and plays. If you expect them to participate in an adult activity then reward them with their own activity of special interest.

- **Move at a child's-pace.** Kidlets move at their own pace and do not tolerate over scheduling. Pay attention to the itinerary.

- **Be educated.** As with adults, the more you can prepare a child for the trip the better the experiences will be. Learning simple foreign phrases, sampling new foods, reading books, and watching movies before your trip will enrich your time together. Role-play going through TSA inspection, customs, and immigration. Make a game of it. There are You-Tube videos to help you.

- **Be entertained.** Most children cannot find things to do on their own. Take a few items that will give you the best bang for your entertainment buck. Skip the expensive electronic device that can be lost or stolen. A box of colored pencils (not crayons – they melt), a pad of paper, a stick of glue, a book, dominos, and a deck of cards provide hours of flexible fun without taking much space or money. Games like Yahztee come in travel-sized versions that I love.

- **Be safe.** Safety is an obvious concern when traveling with children.
  1. Hold hands when crossing streets
  2. Hold hands when embarking or disembarking transportation such as subways
  3. Have contact information on the child. This should include your cellphone and hotel information. Pin it inside their pocket.
  4. Discuss stranger danger to the point you think they have a grasp of it.

- **Be found.** On my trips we call it "being separated from the group," not "lost." It is easy for adults and children to become separated. It only takes a second to turn your head and lose each other. We use the same rules for a person of any age person who becomes separated.
  1. Stop where you are.
  2. Breathe.

3. Stay calm.
4. Wait to be found.
5. We will come back for you.

Have a conversation about asking for help from the police, a mom etc. Be sure you and the child are on the same page with what you feel is best to do. Act out some scenarios until you are both comfortable.

Sharing travel with children is an amazing gift for you and them. Seeing the world at a young age shapes how they see it at an older age. It has the potential to build deep connections between you and with the world. Just do it.

GREEN TRAVEL

Ecologically sensitive travel is a hot topic these days. How can you reduce your "carbon footprint?" How can you help maintain the environment as you travel through it? These are serious questions, and the tourist industry has responded. Hotels tout their green certifications, and tour operators promote eco-holidays and eco-resorts all over the world. A good travel agent can direct you to them.

Eliminate paper brochures by asking for the web addresses of recommended tour companies or hotels. They are probably more current than printed material, anyway. If you do use a brochure, recycle it properly or reuse it by scrapbooking or giving it to a child or school to use for enrichment, reports, or bulletin boards.

Unwrap new items at home where you can properly dispose of packaging materials. There is no reason to take up space and weight in your luggage with the tissue, cardboard, or plastic wrap surrounding your new travel pillow.

When shopping, do what many of you already do at home: **Say "no" to the plastic bag.** Use your purse or tote to carry your purchases or consolidate them into an existing bag. The impact of plastic bags entering landfills is huge. In countries all over the world, I have seen the ghosts of those bags blowing in the wind, floating on the water, and stuck high up in trees.

It may seem too simple, **but use proper receptacles for trash.** Keep garbage in its place, set a good example, and separate yourself from other misbehaving travelers. In some places, including many airports, you will find separate bins for recycling.

Great travel tip: In most European grocery stores, you are expected to bring your own shopping bag and will be charged for one if you don't. The added advantage is that it will have you instantly looking like a local as you carry your purchases. Chicobag makes good ones.

Properly dispose of any spent batteries or other dangerous materials.

One of my personal green travel dilemmas is bottled drinking water. For health reasons, I only drink bottled water when I travel, and it mostly comes in plastic bottles. In a perfect world everyone would have safe drinking water. In the meantime, the **Grayl water filtration system is a super solution.** It is easy to use and has three different levels of filtration. The travel purifying attachment removes the widest variety of contaminants. The Grayl differs from other systems in that it is fast and you can share the pure water with others. I filter in my hotel room, and fill several refillable bottles for the day away from the hotel. My new soft silicone water bottle is a lightweight dream to carry during the day.

Another option is to **buy the largest bottle of water you can carry,** then pour its contents into your own reusable smaller personal bottle for daily use. The other alternative, **water bottled in glass,** is hard to find, heavy to carry, and breakable.

Consider the environmental impact of disposable

items – plastic cups, paper plates, razors, underwear and the like – and think before you throw them out.

Use reusable utensils rather than plastic for your picnics. The sustainable bamboo ones from To-Go Ware even come in a sleeve made from recycled plastic bottles. What is not to like about that?

Follow local rules and signs about walking on the grass or staying on the path. These regulations may protect a fragile eco-system or ensure your safety. In some cities, walking on the park grass is even prohibited.

Do not pick flowers or plants. This can be illegal, dangerous, and with some plants, such as edelweiss and trillium, picking damages them. Some like foxglove and nightshade may look pretty but are toxic or dangerous.

Doing laundry in the hotel sink is often a necessity, but using **earth-friendly products such as Bio Suds** (also mentioned in Chapter 4) makes it less harmful to the environment.

Look for **biodegradable sunscreen and insect repellant**. An estimated 8 million pounds of sunscreen wash into the ocean each year, and four of its common ingredients are thought to be causing damage to fragile coral reefs. Some dolphin encounters and snorkeling or diving excursions require you to wear biodegradable sun products.

Book a hotel with LEED (Leadership in Energy and Environmental Design) certification to know it is being held to a certain level of eco-consciousness.

Hotels all over the world use the same secret code to let you opt out of **the daily towel change.** Hang them up to signal that your will reuse them and leave them on the floor to have them replaced. Why not reuse? Do you wash your towel every day at home? And how often do you need the sheets changed?

Rent a car with the best miles-per-gallon rate. This also saves money on fuel. In some locations you will find hybrid cars available.

Make a mantra of the "Leave No Trace" philosophy of travel. Try to leave any location better than you found it. In places like Antarctica and the Galapagos Islands, even the smallest piece of litter stands out. Reducing our impact is a moral obligation everywhere we go no matter what your politics are.

Strive for only **responsible animal contacts**. Elephant rides, donkey rides, koala encounters, and swimming with dolphins are examples of the types of activities that should be carefully researched.

Purchase **souvenirs that are ecologically correct and legal.** Those that are illegal are so, for a reason. Getting caught with them is criminal, costly, and dangerous, as well as irresponsible. The U.S. State Department Know Before You Go pamphlet is a good resource for understanding the rules and regulations.

CHAPTER 13

Technology and Tools

$\mathcal{W}hen$ YOU OPEN THE DICTIONARY TO "technology," the definition should call it a mixed blessing: We can't live with it, can't live without it. My technology bag is now larger than my makeup bag.

Store all your electronic apparatus – cords, chargers, adapters – in one place. Chargers are the most frequently left behind item in hotel rooms. The good news is that if you leave yours at home, your hotel probably has a "found" one you can borrow! As a reminder, always charge your devices in the same place in the hotel room. My friend Connie suggests making a spot near your toiletry bag so that you're more likely to notice it as you depart.

GET THE PICTURE

Digital photography has made us all into photographers. Wanting to share our experiences graphically via social media is a strong urge for many. Let's explore the equipment to make it happen.

What's your best option for capturing those Kodak moments – a camera with **only a screen on the back or one with a viewfinder?** Those screens can be extremely difficult to use, especially in the bright sun. My preference would be to never again choose a camera without a viewfinder option. However, it can be hard to find a small digital camera with a viewfinder because the camera must be a bit larger than many of the alternatives being offered. But if it's important to you, they are available.

Consider the need to recharge **camera batteries** when traveling abroad or in remote places. Perhaps a camera operating on standard batteries would serve you better than having to recharge a battery.

Each morning, **check the status of the camera's memory and power level.**

Carry extra supplies. Memory cards can be expensive and hard to find when you are away from home. An extra battery and memory card, along with a power pack or portable charger, eliminate the risk of missing photo ops in the course of your day.

Take multiples pictures. In the digital age, we don't have to worry about running out of film or paying to develop a slew of bad photos. Click away, with flash and without, zooming in and out, trying different angles. I do recommend you wait until you get home to do deletions.

Download daily, if you can. You can edit later. I can share sad stories of lost and deleted vacation photos. By downloading them each day to another location, you add a level of safety should your camera be lost or broken.

When traveling with a partner or friend, I encourage **each to carry a camera**. It improves your chance of getting a memorable shot. Serious photographers may want to carry a **small, flexible tripod** to allow for those timed photos and to be included in group shots.

Ditch the rude selfie stick. Those things are a hazard and many places including the Disney parks and Six Flags have outlawed them for good reason.

Do you take vacation pictures for yourself or those back home? Are there times when you are better off leaving the camera behind? Sometimes it's worth savoring the scenery straight on rather than seeing it from behind a lens. Try enjoying being in the moment and just take home your memories.

Camera Etiquette

Carrying a camera carries responsibilities. Good camera manners are important around the world. With the increase of those using iPads or tablets as cameras, this has become especially important. Tablet screens are so big that they block the view of others behind them. One of Murphy's Laws of Travel must be that the person with the extra large iPad always finds his or her way to the front of the group! Please be considerate when using them. And whatever camera you use, let everyone have a turn.

Ask permission to photograph people. Most say yes, but be respectful by allowing them to say no. In Las Vegas I once encountered a very attractive couple in a luxury hotel who made it clear that they did not want to be photographed together. What happens in Vegas stays in Vegas…

What do you do when people demand to be paid for being photographed? There are no easy rules. It is something you must decide for yourself. What is it worth to you? Do you feel like you are being extorted? What are the implications of paying children for a photo when they would be better off in school? Often craftsmen will want to be paid to have you photograph them working. And some artist do not want you to photograph their creative work.

Honor the sensitivities surround religious sites. Churches are amazing repositories of art and architecture. But they are primarily a house of worship. It should be obvious why a family would object to your snapping photos of a funeral of their loved one.

If you promise to send photos to people, do so. Don't break a promise.

Ask permission to post photos of people on social media. It is just common courtesy.

USING YOUR CELL PHONE ABROAD

Our phones have become the Swiss Army knife of life. Their clock, timer, address book, light, voice memos, apps, and camera, provide multiple, important functions. But don't forget: **Cell phones are valuable.** Constantly taking them out to take photos, check the time, perform currency conversion, listen to music, and send messages increases the likelihood that they will be lost or stolen; I know plenty of people for whom this has been the case. A good practice is to carry your cell on a lanyard device. It allows your phone to be readily available and to be tucked into your shirt for security.

The clock on the phone should tell you the proper local time. Check, check, and double-check! I have had trouble with mine being off on occasion. The **alarm and timer** are great for waking you up from a quick nap, reminding you when to take a pill, getting you to the train on time, or waking you in the morning.

The light illuminates a program or menu in dim light or darkness.

Use the notepad or the voice memo feature to hold notes. I use it to remember book titles and historic facts. It can record your daily spending, too.

The phone's camera is useful for recording important facts. **Take a photo of the front of the hotel** to remember the name and to clarify with a taxi driver who may not speak English. **Photograph your room number.** The key card doesn't have the room number on it. After a few nights of moving from city to city, I have trouble remembering my room number. This has created a few humorous moments when I've tried to enter the wrong room. That's a mistake you don't want to make.

Cell phone cameras are now good enough to **take a photo of your daily schedule**. Enlarge it on the screen to view it. I find this helpful on a cruise, where there are so many activities from which to choose and I want the schedule at my fingertips.

The address book on your cell will eliminate having to carry an address book. **Load all necessary addresses and phone numbers** before you leave home. Include the hotel and airline phone numbers and those of any person who may be picking you up or meeting you. This is also a good place to **store frequent flyer numbers** and hotel loyalty membership numbers.

Record your passport data on your phone, including the number and expiration date. I put it in the contact section. It's easier to fill out customs and immigration forms without having to reference your passport. **Take a picture of your passport and email yourself a copy.**

To save paper, **email yourself the itinerary and hotel details.** Include addresses and phone numbers. It is priceless to have all that information at your fingertips.

Phone Calls

This is a field that is changing very fast. For that reason, I cannot give you specific advice. Everyone has a different cellphone and plan and your particular needs are unique. Just know that your best information will come from your carrier.

It is imperative that you contact your service provider to activate international calling, if you need it. At that time you can discuss the range of plans from which you can choose.

There are plans to reduce the very expensive international roaming fees, and for texting and data transmission. On your cell phone you may pay for outgoing and incoming international calls. Your carrier can tell you exactly how to turn off certain functions that incur large costs. I have stored these instructions on my phone to help me remember how to do it each time. If you need to be in contact with home, a **calling card** could be more economical. Purchasing a prepaid local phone is another option as is purchasing a foreign SIM card. Be careful about making any calls from hotel phones; the surcharges are usually huge.

Various **VoIP services** use your computer as a phone. We have FaceTime, Whatsapp, and Skype to name a few of our calling options. We can even see our friends and family on our cell phones while traveling.

Although a cell phone can provide many helpful functions, it is not without complications. Whether you use it or turn it off, it bleeds power. Depending on the age and condition of your battery, even if have turned it off for a week of vacation, it may be out of power by the time you arrive at your home airport and turn it on to call for a ride. Plan on recharging if you are gone for any length of time.

A portable power source is a must. You can charge your phone, camera, or other device even if you are far from an electrical outlet. They are small and relatively inexpensive. It is very easy to deplete power on your cell phone if you are using it as your camera and entertainment source. Having your own power pack is an important backup.

AN ELECTRIFYING SITUATION

Besides currency issues, electricity is the most-asked-about topic among foreign travelers. Converters that change power from one voltage to another and adapters that allow a device to plug into an outlet are necessary in much of the world

Many electronic devices now run on multiple voltages, so they only need an adapter. Look at the very fine print on the plug to see if it says 110-220V. If it does, then it can run on either voltage. You will not need a converter but you will probably need an adapter. For your information, *most* Apple products run on both.

If the item is not dual voltage, you need both the converter and the adapter. The adapter is first plugged into the foreign outlet, then the converter is plugged into the adapter, and then the appliance into the converter. If you don't convert the electricity first, you are likely to see your flat iron melt or your hairdryer become a blow-torch when you turn it on. Luggage stores, travel stores, Batteries Plus, and Radio Shack have experts who can explain what you need and help you find it.

When you travel with multiple items needing power, **think about taking more than one adapter**. They cost just a few dollars and eliminate the stress of waiting for one item to charge before you can plug in another. Yes, I have woken up in the middle of the night to switch items on the adapter.

An extension cord is mandatory when hotels put outlets in odd places. If you use a CPAP machine for sleep apnea, I can almost guarantee the outlet will be on the wrong side of the bed. You still will need an adapter to get the plug of the extension cord to fit into the outlet, but you may plug your appliance right into the extension cord. Get one that has USB and C plugs for maximum adaptability.

You will be the hero when you produce an extension cord in a crowded airport. Outlets are few and far between and when multiple users can share the resource – you have made friends.

THE BEAUTY OF BINOCULARS

A decent pair of binoculars is a must for many itineraries. They enhance your view of theater performances, bring animals closer, and reveal distant mountains more clearly. To me, there is an almost holy communion about sharing my binoculars with the stranger beside me. You can even share them with those who speak another language. As the view becomes larger, the world becomes smaller.

How Do I Choose?

What do those numbers mean? The numbers stamped on the top of a pair of binoculars (for example, 7x35) indicate the magnification and aperture. The (7x) tells how much closer objects will appear. The second number (35) indicates the size of the aperture, which determines how much light the lens takes in. The light determines the brightness of the image, which is important for watching birds at dusk or dawn, stargazing, or theater performances. A high number is less important for viewing roadside geology or glaciers.

How Do I Use Them?

If you wear glasses, keep them on when using binoculars. Adjust the center post so the lenses fit to your eyes. Start with them far apart and then move them closer until you are comfortable.

One side has an adjustable eyepiece. Cover that lens, keeping both eyes open and use the center focusing mechanism to focus on a distant object. With both eyes open, cover the other side and focus that side, using the mechanism on the eyepiece. You are ready to go.

Find an object by pointing at your target with your finger, your eyes will go where your finger points. Or start with a landmark and zero in from there like a treasure map. Move to the left of the tree and up from the rock to whatever you're focusing on. This takes practice! It was only when I went on an African safari that I learned how to use binoculars effectively. There is nothing like that first leopard sighting to motivate you.

CHAPTER 14

Health and Fitness

Travel PUTS STRESS ON OUR BODIES. General good health is required to fight exposure to illness, combat the effects of jet lag, and give us proper mobility. Consider your medical needs early while planning a trip.

PAGING THE DOCTOR

No matter your age or state of health, see your healthcare provider to discuss your travel plans before you embark on a long or exotic trip. This conversation will establish appropriate protocols to deal with existing conditions, combat exposure to disease, and make you more comfortable. Address issues such as visiting high altitudes, jet lag, sleep disturbance, DVT risk assessment, and any problems associated with the food and water. You may be able to handle some of this with a just a phone call. But, if not, consider it the cost of admission to this ride.

Health issues don't have to prohibit travel. Your options may just be more limited. If you have a condition that requires monitoring, work with your medical caregiver on ways to accommodate it. A dear friend on kidney dialysis was able to arrange for her treatments in Hawaii.

Do you take a medication that must be maintained at a constant level? **Talk to the doctor about how to dose as you move around the world.**

SHOTS: SHOOT!

Begin your travels with full knowledge of your immunization status. Check on flu, pneumonia, tetanus, hepatitis, shingles, measles, mumps, whooping cough, tuberculosis, chicken pox, and polio. Because many of these diseases seem to be eradicated in the U.S., it's easy to be lulled into a sense of well-being. Your childhood immunizations may no longer be effective, and immunization recommendations change over time.

Great travel tip: If your primary care physician is not appropriate for advising you on international travel, look for a specialized travel clinic.

Having had a series of polio shots as a child and an oral vaccine later in life, I was cautioned to have a polio booster shot prior to traveling to India, where polio still exists. There are many places where yellow fever, typhoid, cholera, rabies, dengue fever, Japanese encephalitis, and malaria present serious risk. These diseases have the ability to cause permanent damage, lifelong conditions, organ damage, and death but also can all be prevented with proper precautions, medications, or immunizations.

Be the responsible traveler who takes care of herself and protects others. It's not only your health at stake but that of others too. In some countries the public is not immunized to even simple childhood diseases. Given that a single airplane passenger can quickly spread a dangerous disease around the world, we need to be aware of what can happen. And disease can strike anywhere: The state of California reported an epidemic of whooping cough in 2010 and 2014; Washington in 2012 and 2015.

Some oral medication and injections require a certain length of time to achieve full protection, and some require more than one dose, with doses adequately spaced. Medications for malaria and altitude sickness need to be taken for a period of time before they are effective.

Keep a record of your immunizations in the back of your passport. I staple my list to the last page. That is also a good place to record your blood type and allergies.

You MUST wear some form of medical alert item if you have any serious condition or allergy to notify first responders or someone providing first aid. Be sure your travel companion is aware of your situation. For conditions calling for epinephrine, carry it with you at all times and let your travel companions know when and how to administer it. If you are alone, wear your notification 24/7.

Create a basic first aid kit to include remedies for constipation, diarrhea, cold, cough, sore throat, allergy, itching, and indigestion. Add Band-Aids, antibiotic ointment, two aspirins and some moleskin to make a fairly complete kit. I carry mine in a small zippered pouch in my purse. **Minimus.biz** carries most of these in small amounts. Carry just enough for an emergency.

Know the generic name and dosage of your medications. If you run out, lose them, or are seeking medical attention, it is imperative to know the proper

FIRST AID KIT CHECKLIST

- [ ] Bandage selection
- [ ] Moleskin
- [ ] Antibiotic ointment
- [ ] Aspirin
- [ ] Non-aspirin pain reliever
- [ ] Anti-diarrhea medication
- [ ] Stool softener or laxative
- [ ] Day and night cold remedy
- [ ] Cough drops
- [ ] Antihistamine
- [ ] Anti-itch ointment
- [ ] Indigestion remedy
- [ ] Rehydration solution
- [ ] Face mask

generic name and dosage of your medications. The brand names are not the same abroad, and many sound alike. Prilosec and Prozac are two distinctly different drugs, as are Xanax and Zantac. One of my travelers suffered a serious accidental injury. Her treatment was delayed until the doctor could use a cell phone app to determine the generic names of the patient's prescription drugs. The patient remained in pain until it was confirmed that morphine was a safe choice for her.

Great travel tip: Print a list of your conditions, medications, and their dosage. Keep it in the back of your passport. Your pharmacy can provide this information.

If you have a condition requiring injections, take a disposal system to deal with your needles. Needle clippers and disposable containers are available for less than $5. Hotels, planes, trains, and airports do not always have them, and it is irresponsible and dangerous to put used needles in the trash.

SUPER GIRLIE

Women in less developed countries may use newspapers and rags instead of sanitary napkins and tampons, washing them for re-use and hanging them to dry. Young women cannot swim or participate in active play once they begin menstruation. That knowledge certainly gives us a new perspective on our own hygiene habits.

Take a reasonable supply of feminine hygiene products with you. Air travel, jet lag, and stress can upset your menstrual cycle. Have a backup supply in your daily bag for any eventuality. In most urban areas, you can purchase tampons and sanitary napkins similar to those at home. On a day-hike or tour, you could experience an embarrassing emergency.

Discuss with your doctor the potential methods for controlling your cycle for an exotic trip.

If you are visiting India or countries where trash containers aren't readily available, you may want to take some plastic bags in your purse to transport toilet paper, and dispose of sanitary napkins and tampons.

In some cultures, birth control products are readily available, but not in others. Most city pharmacies carry birth control products such as spermicidal creams and condoms. **Take what you need to protect yourself.** Today's smart women travelers don't get caught without supplies to keep themselves safe from sexually transmitted diseases and unwanted pregnancy.

POTTY TALK

Bathrooms and toilet paper differ around the world. Most of them are not as nice as what we expect in the U.S. In Asia and India, you are likely at some time to find a hole in the floor with a place to put your feet while you squat. Believe me, on such occasions, lifting a skirt is much easier than managing your pants around your ankles. Plan your wardrobe accordingly.

One fact remains constant: By the time you've navigated the ladies room queue with your legs crossed, the toilet paper will be gone. Books and packing lists tell you to pack your own small roll of toilet tissue. That good advice, but if it is in your purse, you may have to perform a circus balancing act to reach it in the small stall.

In many countries, women make their living keeping the restroom more or less clean and supplied. The job may consist of handing you a paper towel or tissue. But

Great travel tip: Stash a small amount of tissue in the waist of your panties. Fold it really flat. It won't add much bulk around your middle. And when you need it it will be in the right place at the right time.

THE OFT MISUNDERSTOOD BIDET

That second thing in the bathroom that resembles a toilet, is the bidet. It is not meant for soaking your feet or chilling your champagne bottle. Its function is to cleanse your genital and anal area. There, we have said it. So how is it used?

Once you know its purpose you will find recognizable parts on it. There is a spray, a drain, hot and cold control knobs and a knob to set the flow of the water. Try it. You may become a convert to it.

Here are the step by step instructions:

1. Use the toilet first.

2. Squat/sit/hover over the bidet. It does not have a toilet seat on it. You sit/squat or hover over the cold bowl. You may face forward or backward. It may be easier to face the controls for your first attempt. This usually necessitates removing your pants and underwear.

3. Note from where the spray is going to originate. It is possible that there is not a sprayer, but the bidet just fills with water which you then splash on yourself. Modern bidets are also sometimes incorporated as a part of the toilet, especially in Asia where space is limited.

4. Turn on the water with the hot and cold control knobs, beginning with the cold. You don't want to burn yourself. Adjust it to a comfortable temperature.

5. Set the spray force with the third knob. It could come from the back or the bottom of the bidet. Take this step slowly. Sometimes a small movement of that knob makes a big adjustment. You could be spraying the ceiling of the bathroom. You might hold your hand over the sprayer until you determine its velocity.

6. After what you deem as adequate cleansing, dry off with the small towel that is usually hung nearby.

7. Rinse out the bidet.

8. Wash your hands with soap and water. Walk out with a smile on your face and proudly proclaim to your friends that you have mastered the bidet.

no matter what you think of the service, **give her a small coin and a smile.** It's not going to blow your budget.

Not all countries have plumbing capable of accepting toilet paper, much less tampons. If you are in a third-world or developing country, or if you question the abilities of the plumbing, **use the covered trashcan sitting beside the toilet for all products.** This is quite common in many places. If the toilet is of the squatting variety mentioned above, the paper always goes in a receptacle. In fact, these kinds of toilets rarely even come with toilet paper. BYO. Be warned, sometimes there is not a trashcan, or it located outside the toilet enclosure. This is when it is handy to have a Ziploc bag stashed in your purse.

In some cultures, the reason people eat with their right hand and never their left is because the left is used with a splash of water to clean themselves in the bathroom. This is why you may see a hose and pitcher or bucket in the toilet stall. I have not adopted this local skill, nor do I intend to. Now you know.

The bathroom is one of those places where your cotton bandana is likely to come in handy. Use it to dry your hands when there are no towels. If there is a communal cloth towel you will be especially glad to have your bandana.

FITNESS ON THE ROAD

Gyms and workout rooms are common in upscale hotels. You also can take your own equipment to use in any hotel room; for example, **Dyna-Bands and Thera-Bands** are small and cost less than $10. Plenty of online sites demonstrate exercises to perform with them.

If you prefer free weights, use a one-liter water bottle to

approximate a 1.5 pound weight. Or try some isometric moves. You are NOT going to pack weights!

If you take to the streets or trails alone for a run or walk, **tell someone where you are going and when you will return. Carry ID and the address of your hotel.** Be sure you know where you are going and return before dark. Let someone know if your plans change.

STAYING WELL ON THE ROAD

Nothing is more miserable than being sick away from home. Even a cold is wretched, but to be seriously ill can be frightening and dangerous.

Travel compromises your immune system. The lack of regular sleep, changing time zones, irregular meal times, fast food, shortage of dietary fiber, dehydration, and stress assault your body. The best defense is prevention.

Eat regular meals and eat as healthfully as possible. Fruits, vegetables, and fiber are necessary for good health anywhere. For those times when your appetite is on a different schedule, eat a granola bar or other snack to take the edge off your hunger. Any packaged snack will do if you can't get something fresh. Carry something with you especially if you are prone to blood sugar problems.

Stay hydrated with CLEAN water, especially in warm climates or with exertion. Water is an important element in the recipe for good health. Carry clean water so you are never forced to drink anything not pure. Travelers can have intestinal problems anywhere as a result of different water. Use the Grayl filter mentioned in Chapter 12.

Tie your bandana, a ribbon, or a rubber band on the tap or faucet handle to remind you not to drink from it.

The most widely accepted method for avoiding Traveler's

Diarrhea is to employ the mantra: **BOIL IT, COOK IT, PEEL IT, OR FORGET IT.** It is impossible to confirm how food has been prepared or stored when eating out. You will have to trust that proper guidelines are being met. When you purchase an apple from a vendor, peel it with your clean knife, or instead choose a banana that you can peel more easily. Lettuce salads have not been peeled or cooked and should be avoided, along with uncooked cabbage. Dairy products can be a source of intestinal problems. Eat only pasteurized products. Your doctor may suggest a course of Pepto Bismol while you travel. Better ask about it.

My friend Sharon orders a cup of hot water in a restaurant. She figures it has been boiled and will be less expensive than ordering the $5 bottled water. This practice got her through Peru and Ecuador in good health.

Be compulsive about hand washing when you travel. I regularly encounter women who worry about becoming ill on a trip, yet at lunch they dip into the communal bread basket without washing their hands. Don't! Every doorknob, hand railing, and subway strap is teeming with germs. The first thing to do before eating anything, including an ice cream cone, is to clean your hands.

If soap and water is not available, use a hand sanitizer. You can find this product in various appealing fragrances if you prefer. **Antibacterial wipes are handy for cleaning germs off of**

Great travel tip: Ice might be made from tap water. Unless you know it to be from purified water, avoid it. That goes for the blended margaritas, too, chicas. Sorry, alcohol does not kill the germs!

Great travel tip: Germophobes take heed- When traveling in Asia, take an extra pair of socks to wear when you must remove your shoes for temple visits.

hard surfaces like airplane trays, toilet seats, remote controls, and telephones.

After you've washed your hands in the ladies room, use a paper towel to turn the doorknob on the way out, then toss it or stick it in your bag. Where paper towels are not available, you have your bandana. You are such a savvy traveler!

Here Comes the Sun

Protecting your skin by blocking the sun's UV rays either chemically or physically is important to avoid wrinkles and skin cancer. If you prefer better living through chemistry, realize that sunblock **must be used liberally and frequently**. Don't miss your ears, the back of your neck, hands, and tops of your feet. According to the American Academy of Dermatologists, you need to use one ounce, enough to fill a shot glass, to cover the exposed areas of the body properly. Remember, lips get sunburned, too, so apply a lip balm containing sunscreen with a good SPF.

Protect your skin by physical barriers. Covering up with any clothing will help. Check out **Coolibar,** a company with a commitment to providing a wide variety of protective clothing and accessories. It can be found online.

Wear a hat. Visors do not offer the same protection as a good hat because the open top allows your scalp to burn. A hat should be woven tightly enough to protect you but offer enough ventilation to be cooling.

Sunscreens should be reapplied about every two hours and after swimming or perspiring heavily. Even so-called "water-resistant" sunscreens lose effectiveness after 40 minutes in the water. Sunscreens rub off and wash off. If you've towel-dried, you need to reapply sunscreen for continuing protection.

Sunscreens lose their potency with time. **Check the expiration date**, and if the container doesn't show one, toss it after three years. **Use a tried-and-true product when you travel**. Make sure you don't have sensitivity to it before you ruin your tropical vacation with a rash.

Stay cool by moving to the shade. Try a fan and look glamorous, too. It worked for Cleopatra! Or place a cold water bottle on the back of your neck or chest. My friend Carol partially fills a plastic bottle with water and freezes it. As it melts, it provides cool water. Another friend, Sue, uses a wet bandana around her neck to chill out. These cool ladies live in Oklahoma City and New Orleans, respectively, so they know what it takes to beat the heat.

Parasols or umbrellas create shade and are cute. They do not provide protection for your skin.

Mesh is breathable, but it doesn't provide sun protection. You sure do not want a mesh patterned sunburn on your back.

Stay hydrated by drinking water. Water sprayed on the skin provides a quick cool-down. The Evian Brumisateur spray I love comes in a travel size. You can also take your own small spray bottle and fill it with water. Add a drop of essential oil for added aromatherapy benefits.

Seasick Yuck

If you have a propensity to motion sickness; load up an arsenal. **You need to be ahead of the game.** Conquering it after you feel unwell is nearly impossible. You must be proactive. A ginger candy may calm a slightly queasy stomach for some. Others have luck with Sea-Bands™ or another natural acupressure device worn on the wrist, as an alternative to medications. If needed, be prepared to bring out the big guns of **Dramamine™, Bonine™ or**

a non-drowsy version thereof. If you know you suffer with these issues, you probably have a favorite remedy. Be supplied and ready to use it. Will moving to the front seat help, or looking out to the horizon?

You Bug Me

Bugs carry life-threatening diseases. The American Mosquito Control Association says that over 1 million people die each year from mosquito-borne illnesses, including malaria, dengue, yellow fever, West Nile virus, chikungunya, and zika virus. Although inoculations and medications can prevent some of those illnesses, the first line of defense is to keep the darned buzzing beasts off you.

- **Form protective barriers** so that mosquitos can't get to you. Long sleeves, long pants, socks to cover the ankles, and sleeping under a mosquito net will do the trick.

- **Wear clothes permeated with the chemical permethrin** to keep the bugs at bay. One of the popular brands is Buzz Off. Permethrin also comes as a spray to use on your own clothing.

- **Use an effective repellent such as DEET or picaridin.** I don't like using chemicals on my skin any more than most people, but they are effective in the war on mosquitos. DEET is the old stand-by, picaridin a more recent, non-greasy invention, but both are considered safe for human use. My favorite travel doctor recommends Ultrathon, which contains a high level of DEET and lasts as long as 12 hours. It is available as a pump, spray, or lotion. There are other herbal and natural methods that can be explored but are not shown to be as effective.

THIS IS AN EMERGENCY

Traveling forces us to be very self-sufficient. We must be able to independently discern when we need extra help and when we can go it alone.

Women's Heart Health

Women's heart attack symptoms can differ from those of men. Know the symptoms and heed them. According to the American Heart Association, they are:

Chest discomfort. Most heart attacks involve discomfort in the center of the chest that lasts more than a few minutes or that goes away and comes back. It can feel like uncomfortable pressure, squeezing, fullness, or pain.

Discomfort in other areas of the upper body. Symptoms can include pain or discomfort in one or both arms, the back, neck, jaw, or stomach.

Shortness of breath with or without chest discomfort.

Other signs may include breaking out in a cold sweat, feeling light-headed, or experiencing nausea.

As with men, women's most common heart attack symptom is **chest pain or discomfort**. But women are somewhat more likely than men to experience some of the other common symptoms, particularly **shortness of breath, nausea/vomiting, and back or jaw pain**.

New guidelines are in place to treat potential **heart attacks**.

PEARLY WHITES HIT THE ROAD

Chances are, the same exotic place where mosquitos hang out also will have a limited supply of clean water. Here's how to **brush your teeth when purified water is scarce:**

Two-Tablespoon Toothbrushing

- Pour water into glass.
- Apply toothpaste to brush.
- Brush your teeth.
- Take one sip to rinse.
- Swish toothbrush in glass to clean.
- Toss out water and you are done.

To avoid leaving your toothbrush in a hotel bathroom, get a holder with a suction cup that attaches to the mirror. It's hard to ignore it hanging on the mirror. If you cannot live without your electric toothbrush, expect it to go a week or more without recharging. Test yours and see.

1. **Call 911 or the emergency number for your location.** Fast response is critical.
2. **Administer aspirin if directed by 911 personnel.** Add them to your purse now. I love Aspirinpod, a cute, heart-shaped container that can attach to your key ring, to keep your aspirin close at hand. Find them at aspirinpod.com and get one for everyone you love.
3. **Look for an Automated External Defibrilator (AED).** They are self-directing and very easy to use.
4. **Prepare to administer CPR** if the person arrests. To establish the proper cadence, sing along with the Bee Gees to that disco classic "Stayin' Alive."

Hiking through the rainforest in Costa Rica, my You Go Girls! group ran into a very distressed man racing down the trail toward us. He asked if any of us had two aspirin, and I gave him mine. He turned and ran back up the trail. A while later we encountered his hiking party carrying out one of their members. The man was clearly having a heart attack; his skin was gray and he was moaning in pain. Fortunately, the three doctors in his group had administered the aspirin, his heart did not arrest, and they assured us that we'd helped save his life, all because of those pills in my pocket.

One Stroke and You're Out

Do you know the signs of a stroke? The single most important action in the event of a stroke is to get help IMMEDIATELY. According to the National Institute of Neurologic Disorders and Stroke (NINDS), the first 60 minutes are critical to prevent disability. **Get help as soon as possible.** NINDS lists stroke symptoms as:

- **Sudden numbness or weakness** of the face, arm, or leg (especially on one side of the body).
- **Sudden confusion**, trouble speaking, or trouble understanding speech.
- **Sudden trouble seeing** in one or both eyes.
- **Sudden trouble walking**, dizziness, loss of balance, or coordination.
- **Sudden severe headache** with no known cause.

Great travel tip: For exotic trips, talk to your doctor about an antibiotic for serious conditions.

The National Stroke Association offers the following mnemonic trick for recognizing a stroke:

- **F**ace – Ask the person to smile. Does one side of the face droop?
- **A**rms – Ask the person to lift both arms. Does one drift downward?
- **S**peech – Ask the person to repeat a simple phrase. Is the speech slurred or strange?
- **T**ime – If you observe ANY of these signs, call 911 and get emergency help immediately.

YOU MAKE ME SICK

If you do become ill while away, consult a doctor. Any reputable hotel will be able to connect you to an English-speaking doctor. If you are not comfortable consulting the hotel, call the U.S. Embassy to find one. In some locales they are not expensive, and in others they are outrageous, but your health and comfort are priceless.

Take someone with you if you need to

Great travel tip: If illness or injury forces you to interrupt your vacation or to be evacuated, you will be grateful for the travel insurance discussed in Chapter 2. Most offer an emergency helpline as a benefit.

see a doctor. Two heads are better than one, communication may be difficult, and a woman should consider the need to be accompanied in a situation where a strange man may be examining her. This can be a big cultural gap.

If you develop a gastric or intestinal problem that involves vomiting or diarrhea, there is real danger of **becoming dehydrated**. Ask your doctor before you leave home what guidelines to follow, what complications to be aware of, and whether you need antibiotics for the trip. In some cases letting the problem run its course is best, and in others it's better to intervene.

Digestive issues seem to fall into three categories.

1. Simple tummy aches that go away or can be controlled by something such as Pepto Bismol.
2. Traveler's diarrhea that needs intervention with an Imodium type drug.
3. Serious diarrhea that lasts several days, becomes bloody or is accompanied by a fever. This is a more serious condition that may require a prescriptive solution.

Have a plan in place in the event a problem does arise. **Bring contact information for your doctor, dentist, and pharmacy with you.** Discuss the BRAT (Banana, Rice, Applesauce, Toast) diet with your doctor as well as rehydrating options. You can purchase rehydrating packets or make your own.

Rehydration mix:
1/2 teaspoon of salt
6 teaspoons of sugar
1 liter of purified water

Colds, earaches, toothaches, and flying do not mix. You must see a doctor before you board a plane with any of these conditions. You risk your hearing, health, and great discomfort to fly. Eardrums burst, and infections from ears and teeth can spread.

CHAPTER 15

Keeping It All Together

People ARE GENERALLY GOOD, AND MOST places are generally safe. But we also must be smart about protecting ourselves. Even though women are more vulnerable than men, we are also smart and capable of learning how to take care of ourselves. We also watch out for each other.

Be aware of your surroundings. This is the cardinal rule of personal safety anywhere. Carrying too many pieces of luggage or bags is distracting. Having full hands creates an appearance of helplessness. When you're in a strange place, you don't want to be beholden to a stranger who has offered assistance.

Look like you know where you are going. Plan your route. If you need to consult the map, step against a wall or into a shop to get your bearings. **Ask a shopkeeper, police officer, or another woman for help. A word to the wise - In some places there are tourist police as well as municipal police.** Do your homework to confirm that police are your best resource in a certain

Country. I have had an over-enthusiastic tourist officer volunteer to direct me to shops that were obviously giving him a kickback.

Know the address of where you are staying and some local landmarks to keep taxi drivers from taking advantage of you. When you leave your hotel, be sure to take a business card or matchbook with the hotel name, address, and phone number on it. Mark it on your map and enter it into your cell phone.

Use only officially authorized taxis. *Never* accept a ride from anyone else. Settle on a price before entering a cab. Either it is a metered plan or a prearranged price. Your hotel concierge, reception staff, or doorman can give you an approximate cost to expect. When you leave a cab, **check the floor and seat to be sure you have not left any items behind**. I'm pretty casual about taxis, but it is a good idea to at least note the company name of the taxi in case you leave something behind.

In countries where there are frequent kidnappings for ransom, use only taxis procured by a hotel. Do not hail them on the street. Ecuador is just one popular tourist destination with a history of such kidnappings.

Watch your drink. In the '70s, women worried about someone dropping LSD or acid into their drink. All drinks are vulnerable – your cocktail, beer, or wine in addition to your iced tea, soft drink, water, or coffee. The current danger is a potent date rape drug known as roofies, or gamma-Hydroxybutyric acid (GHB). Never leave your drink unattended. Finish it before heading to the ladies room or dance floor. No age group is immune from this risk. This is a potential threat in bars, pubs, cruise ships, coffeehouses, and airplanes. The stranger beside you is just that, a stranger, and some strangers are stranger than others.

Keep an eye on your valuables. Personal belongings are even at risk on the plane. If you must leave them unattended, ask for help from the flight attendant. Your money, passport, cell phone, etc. are valuable enough for someone to steal.

As a solo traveler, you need to check in with someone on a regular basis. It could be an email to a certain person at home or a call to a family member at an appointed time. I've wondered how long I could disappear before someone would become alarmed. Any good friend should be happy to serve as your touch-point while you are gone.

Luggage Locks

You can spend $20 on a luggage lock if it makes you feel better. In my experience they disappear in the TSA screening, never to be seen again, and I kiss my money goodbye. A zip tie is about as effective. At least, you will know if someone was in your bag. Some sort of lock may serve as a slight deterrent in a hostel, but your best defense is to not put anything of value in your bag.

COUNTDOWN 1-2-3

Here is a simple method to prevent losing things along the way. As you begin your day or go out, count what you have with you. With each transition you make during the day, count again to be sure you have everything. My refrain goes something like this: *purse, camera, scarf, coat*. The fewer items you have to keep track of, the better.

Check your surroundings when you leave any location. Whether getting off the subway, leaving a restaurant, or checking out of a hotel, do a quick review. Cameras, sunglasses, purses, scarves, umbrellas, and gloves are some of the obvious items that are easily left behind.

A place for everything and everything in its place. If

your passport is always in the same place, you will never have that momentary panic of thinking it is lost – unless, of course, it really is. Putting your things back in the same place allows you to relax and save time looking for lost items. Ignore the person behind you giving you a dirty look while you take an extra few seconds to stow things where they belong. It will save you hours of frustration later.

A client showed her passport to board the plane. She carried it with her newspaper and coffee onto the plane where she put her bag in the overhead bin, took off her coat, sat down with her coffee, and settled in for her flight. Fast-forward to the next connection, where she found her passport missing. It could have been stolen, left in the seat pocket, dropped on the floor, or thrown away with the newspaper. This led to two extra nights in Chicago awaiting a new passport, paying to expedite that passport, and missing two days in Paris.

Do things the same way. Each time you check out of a hotel, check under the beds (use your flashlight), and make one last check of the closet, drawers, and bathroom for items left behind. Don't forget the shower. Pull back the shower curtain and directly look into it, high and low. Start at the point farthest from the door and work your way out, making one last check along the way.

When I have an early departure, I have my bag ready to go the night before. I put the clothes I will need in the morning, including underwear and accessories, onto one hanger. To remember things left in the refrigerator or to return an extension cord to the reception desk, I put a reminder note on the door.

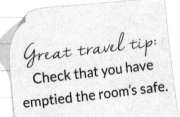

Great travel tip:
Check that you have emptied the room's safe.

Valuables

Items you don't want to lose should not travel with you. That may include the inexpensive but favorite necklace your niece made you or a valuable heirloom diamond ring. If you need your bling, be sure it is something you can afford to lose. Expensive jewelry is an obvious risk, but this warning extends to everything, including your clothing. How will you feel if your brand new designer cashmere sweater disappears between Atlanta and Minneapolis?

Great travel tip: Confirm the location of your passport the DAY BEFORE you need it to return home or cross another border.

Protect yourself by not flaunting valuables. Losing an item is one thing. Being robbed or mugged is traumatic. Cell phones and cameras are attractive targets. So are passports, credit cards, cash, and jewelry.

If you want to wear a wedding ring, get a simple substitute. I found a gold travel ring on eBay that's more comfortable in hot weather than my diamond wedding ring.

Hiding valuables is not an effective loss prevention plan. I know of many situations where hidden cash and jewelry have disappeared from hotel rooms and bags. Yes, they will find that wad of cash stashed in your toiletry bag. You are not going to outsmart them.

PURSE SAFETY

We've talked about choosing a good travel handbag and how to carry it cross-body. In a restaurant, it is best **kept on your lap, under your control.** Do not hang it on your chair back or set it on an adjacent chair, free for the taking. I have seen a purse taken off the floor of a Laundromat. I was in the pub when one was snatched off a booth by someone who reached it from under the

Great travel tip: Leave the extra credit cards, library card, pizza punch cards, and gym membership card at home. Extra keys should stay home, too. If you don't need them, don't take them. It will lighten your load.

adjacent booth. A woman sitting at the bar next to my son's date was caught on videotape deliberately scooping up the young woman's purse. This happens all the time here and abroad.

Wallet Leash

Some travel purses come with what I call a **wallet leash**. This is a strap that is internally connected to the bag and has a clasp to attach to your wallet. It should keep your wallet from being easily removed from your bag by a pickpocket.. If your bag does not have one, you can buy one from my website.

RFID and More

News of disasters, rip-offs, and threats permeate our Facebook pages and news feeds, causing us to create new ways to secure our possessions. Now another threat rears its ugly head – RFID. What the heck is that? RFID stands for Radio Frequency Identification. It is a way to hold and transmit data like a bar code or a magnetic strip. Your new credit card probably has an RFID chip. Your passport does too. It can be tracked and read with a special reader.

Your security is compromised when an unscrupulous person decodes information without your knowledge. Yes, they can scan your data from a distance without you even knowing. With this mined information, they are able to steal your identity and potentially access your financial data. The chances are small but they are there. If any of this is a serious worry to you it is easy to protect yourself with RFID blocking products.

Alternately, carrying them in a metal box

Great travel tip: Museums, galleries, and historic sites may ask you to check your bag. Be prepared with your wallet and anything important secured in a smaller bag that can be removed and taken with you. That should keep them secure in a communal bag check.

(from your old throat lozenges) or wrapping them in foil will accomplish the same thing, but that might look silly. Wallets, handbags, and money belts are on the market to provide RFID protection to a variety of vulnerable items. Now you will know what they are when you see them advertised.

Yes, there are also people out there who might slash your handbag or cut its handle. As for steel cables imbedded in the handles of handbags and slash-proof fabrics, my stand may differ from that of many. Let them slash away. I have nothing of value in that bag. If purchasing such a bag will make you feel good, then get one. BUT do not allow it to be a license to be careless. You know better.

Great travel tip: No self-respecting woman wants the appearance of an extra 10 pounds on the tummy. Spin the belt around so the pouch is tucked in at the small of your back. Nobody will notice it there.

Choosing and Using a Money Belt

Money belts or personal safes come in various styles. They are worn around the neck or waist, over the shoulder, around the ankle, or on a bra. They are made from cotton, silk, nylon, mesh, and other materials. Choose one based on climate and comfort, then USE IT.

The waist models are not easily accessible if you are wearing a dress. The neck models are visible when wearing skimpier clothing in warm climates. Take the version that will accommodate your wardrobe. That could mean taking a selection for various outfits.

Tissues, sunglasses, guidebook, map, granola bar, first aid kit, and makeup belong in your purse; **valuables do not.** Be secure in knowing thieves will get nothing of value, even if they get your purse. **Carry a small amount of cash for the day and one credit card in a secure pocket or handbag.** Carry backup funds and cards in your money belt. Avoid revealing your money belt in public places where others can see your stash.

Passports and large amounts of cash must be safe against your body. If someone wants them, they will have to strip you. When valuables are not in clear sight, criminals will look for an easier target.

In Ecuador I was the victim of a mugging. Six of us were briskly walking to our hotel after dinner. A young man charged toward me and stripped the necklace right off my neck. If any of us had been dangling a purse from our shoulder, I am sure he would have taken that. He took the necklace because it was easy, but it wasn't valuable. I had purchased it in Peru for $35. None of us were carrying a handbag; instead, we had our Scottevest travel vests and money belts. Having a purse yanked off your shoulder is likely to hurt you. Losing large amounts of cash, credit cards, passport, or valuable jewelry carried in your purse would be a terrible loss.

Your **passport is the single most important and valuable possession you carry when you travel.** Losing it is a big problem.

Keep your passport on your body. Should you have an accident or be caught in a disaster, you will need it. Don't leave it in your room, and don't carry it in your purse. **Carry it in some sort of money belt against your body at all times.** If you are going swimming at the beach, you may leave it in the safe at the hotel where it will be secure.

Many books tell you to carry a **photocopy of your passport** to facilitate replacement of a lost one. I recommend that you also take a photo of it with your phone. Having this done will not automatically replace a lost one, as a copy cannot be used in place of the original. You must be issued a new one. One of my experiences with a lost passport taught me that in today's electronic world, the government already knows who you are and where you are but it certainly won't hurt to have a photocopy. Copy the front page with the basic information and any visa pages that apply to this particular trip. Keep the duplicate in a safe place separate from your passport.

A client lost her passport between the hotel and lunch in Galway, Ireland. After searching high and low, we began hatching a plan to get her back to Dublin to replace it. This little bump in the road was going to cause her to miss her flight home the next day. The cost was increasing by the minute as we considered train tickets, passport photos, passport fees, taxis, a hotel room for the night, and a fee to change her airline ticket.

Fortunately, the taxi driver who had delivered her to lunch had given her his business card. After several calls to the taxi company and multiple pleas from the dispatcher to the fleet of drivers, the driver was located and found her passport in the back seat of his car. When he returned it to her at the hotel, she gave him a big hug and a kiss. He refused a tip. You have to love the Irish.

Two profitable lessons were learned that day. Her passport had been in her purse, and when she took out cash for the taxi fare, it had fallen out. This is exactly why it belongs in your money belt. Secondly, I now try to note the name of the taxi company.

LOST IN LONDON

Part of the fun of travel is getting lost. It makes for good stories. It's said you haven't truly explored Venice, Italy, until you've been lost there. If you think getting lost *will not* enhance your vacation, these hints should keep you on the right track.

Know the name and address of your hotel. As mentioned earlier, carry a business card, matchbook, or **digital photo of the front of the hotel.**

If you're in a country with a different alphabet or one that uses different characters, be sure to **have important information written for you using that set of characters.** Greece, Japan, Thailand, Russia, China, and many other countries fall into this category.

Use a map. Buy them *before* you travel. Once at your destination, look for them at the local tourism office, the airport, and at your hotel's reception desk. Try the GPS on your phone or download maps onto it. Just watch your data usage if you are abroad.

Ask the front desk staff or concierge to give you directions before you go out. When you believe you have gone in a wrong direction, **stop and ask before you get hopelessly frustrated and frightened.** Stay calm and look for solutions. Remember your Girl Power!

Carry a compass. I like the ones that clip on to a zipper and also have a thermometer. You can find one on your cell phone too. At the very least, it shows you which direction to exit the subway. As you exit what feels like the center of the earth, it's sometimes difficult to know which exit to use. The compass will send you in the proper direction.

My husband and I got so turned around in the French countryside once that only a compass got us headed back on track. Wherever we were, it was a memorable experience: A lovely old Frenchman presented me with a bouquet of flowers he had obviously picked from the neighbor's yard. A World War II survivor, he wanted to express his gratitude to an American. On that day, I was the fortunate recipient for his thanks. Getting lost rewarded both of us with a special memory.

People learn in different styles. Some are auditory learners, some are visual, and some are kinetic. A map may be more helpful to a visual person, and verbal directions may be better for an auditory learner. Know what works for you and play to your strength.

Do what you need to do to get yourself off in the right direction from the start.

HOTEL SAFETY

You have done everything in your power to ensure you are staying at a reputable hotel in a safe area. Sites with independent reviews like TripAdvisor supply insight from previous guests' experiences. Your professional travel agent is also a reliable resource. Now it is your responsibility to remain safe.

To review the basics:

- **Never admit a stranger into your room.**
- **Keep your room number secure.**
- **Place a doorstop wedge under your door if you feel vulnerable to intruders.**
- **Interior halls are safer** than those opening to a parking lot or street.
- **Higher floors are safer** than the ground floor.
- **Check the locks on your hotel doors and windows and use them.** Be sure to check balcony or patio doors. This simple first line of defense is often the most effective.

How many times have I heard the reception clerk loudly give a woman her room number in front of other guests? Everyone in the lobby doesn't need to know that Ms. Miller is alone in room 421. Ditch that room and say, "Will you please give me another room without revealing the number to the people standing behind me?" Or, "I am uncomfortable with the people behind me knowing my room number. Please give me a new one." What would you teach your daughter to do? Treat yourself as well as you would have her demand to be treated. Hotel employees are getting better about the needs of women travelers, but sometimes they just forget. Help them remember and move on with a thank you.

Do not allow yourself to be in the room alone with hotel staff. If a man comes to deliver room service, use your doorstop to prop the door open. Use your coat or robe to cover up if you are not dressed properly. Report any improprieties to management immediately.

Have a working cell phone to call for help and know what number to dial in an emergency. In other countries it might not be 911.

Use the safe to secure items, but realize that the hotel does have the ability to open it in your absence. More hotels are putting in safes to hold full-sized laptops. That's nice.

If you are traveling alone, **tell the desk staff when and where you're going and when to expect your return.** This is important day or night. Let them know if you change plans.

Do not use the door hanger to ask for the room to be serviced. That is a signal that you are gone from the room. Call housekeeping to request service if you need it outside of the scheduled time. Hanging the Do Not Disturb sign on the door is not a bad idea; that makes it look like you *are* in the room.

Once you are safely in your room, there are some very important things to know and remember. Arm yourself to possibly save your own life. Incorporating these simple habits will free you from fear.

Know your way out. Take a minute and note the emergency escape route. Count the steps or doors to the exit.

I was once sound asleep in a hotel when the maid woke me up by pounding on the door and shouting "FIRE." The hall smelled of smoke. My mother's voice echoed in my head, warning me not use the elevator. In my nightgown I made my way to the nearest stairs and down to a lobby full of completely dressed guests. As it turned out, a kitchen fire in an adjacent hotel had blown smoke through an open window and into our hall. We were safe. But I headed back to bed with my adrenaline still pumping.

I have also experienced false alarms in a high-rise Las Vegas hotel, especially frightening with that city's history of fatal hotel fires. I repeat: **Knowing where to go eliminates anxiety, allowing you to respond quickly when it could mean your life.**

Keep shoes by the bed for a quick emergency exit. Broken glass is a potential danger. Slip on those shoes as you exit.

Know what to do in an earthquake. Drop, cover, and hold on. Drop means to stay low, cover means getting under a desk or table. Stay away from glass and any tall items likely to tip or drop. Running into the street may be your first inclination, but falling debris makes that potentially unsafe. If you are in bed, stay there, cover your head with a pillow and hold on. Be prepared that alarms will be sounding and power may be interrupted.

Whoever would have thought we would be having a conversation about what to do in a hotel terrorist attack? The chances of this are slim. Security experts suggest it is something for which you cannot prepare because each situation is so unique. Law enforcement tells us the best course of action is to **barricade yourself in your room.** This is not a time for confrontation or heroism. If they rattle your door and find it secured, hope they move down the hall to an easier target.

ADDRESSING SAFETY

Do not wear anything showy. Criminals do not know the difference between real and fake. They will cut off your finger for a big fake as easily as for the real deal. **The only safe items are the ones you leave at home in the safe or safe deposit box at the**

bank. Dressing to not call attention to yourself will help prevent you from being a target.

Red, White and Blue; Christian or Jew

I'm proud to be an American. I'm lucky, by accident of birth, to be an American. I don't want to deny being an American, but I am cautious and recognize the whole world does not view the U.S. approvingly. Negative attitudes are usually directed to our government and not at us personally, but personal safety is not to be compromised.

Keep your passport in a cover to conceal your citizenship. You will be asked by the inspector to remove it, but nobody else needs to see it.

Do not wear clothing with American logos, stars and stripes, or flags.

Don't wear religious jewelry. I am a Christian and at home wear a gold cross on a necklace. As an American traveling abroad, it is simply foolish to announce your religion. It can be extremely inflammatory. Flaunting your faith, whatever it is, could cost your life. I recognize this is a difficult stance for those who feel called to share their faith. Be aware of what it could mean in the context of modern world politics. And when traveling in a group, consider what it might cost others too. Do you remember the *Achille Lauro* hijacking when wheelchair-bound Leon Klinghoffer was murdered and pushed into the ocean for being Jewish? This is the reality of our world. In order to travel safely, you must adjust to it.

Maintain a low profile by using a quiet voice and appropriate behavior.

Do not be overly demanding.

Avoid demonstrations, political gatherings, or riots. You do not know when a group will turn violent or the police or military may step in. You probably do not have a stake in the discussion or knowledge of the issue. Whether the issue appears to be domestic or international – STAY AWAY. You do not need to be in the middle of it.

I have seen sweet little Italian men put up quite a fight regarding increasing their pensions. Even situations that seem to be peaceful can turn quickly, putting you in danger.

CANNABIS, CBD, THC AND MORE

As many states in the U.S. adopt new laws regarding cannabis products. These changes may have fostered a new complacency around their uses. Your casual use of gummies to enhance sleep, CBD oil for your bum knee, or a low THC joint to relieve the stress of flying may be perfectly legal at home, but they bring new questions as you travel.

Firstly, know that any and all cannabis use or procession is illegal according to the U.S. federal government. States have legislated laws unique to each of them, but in the eyes if the U.S., it is still illegal. As a result, state lines and international borders present major stumbling blocks to the transportation of these products. It is against Federal law to transport ANY AND ALL marijuana products across state lines, even when it is legal to possess them in your state or a state you are entering or exiting. The other important encounter you can expect to be problematic is with the T.S.A. While they are not charged with policing drug traffic and they are not searching for cannabis, they are a part of the government. They are required to report drug procession to law enforcement. You are risking criminal prosecution if you are found to be carrying marijuana or cannabis products onto an airplane in the U.S., even within a state that has legalized them.

Countries of the world have their statutes, and the privilege of U.S. citizenship will not help you in fighting them. Some, like the Netherlands are quite open and liberal. Others, like Singapore, Malaysia, and Turkey are very intolerant. Many others are experiencing changes similar to those of the U.S. states. Suspicion, use, or possession can be a serious offense exposing you to harsh and inhumane punishments. As always - their country, their rules.

It is your responsibility to remain cautious. There are people out there who are paid to set you up to be caught in possession of dangerous substances. Avoid being a victim by not accepting any drugs from anyone when you travel. My clients were approached in a Mexican resort town to purchase marijuana. They politely declined and continued their walk around the corner, where police were waiting. They were certain that the police were waiting to catch them red handed with the pot.

LOSING YOUR LUGGAGE

High on the list of the World's Worst Travel Problems is lost luggage or a lost passport.

Curse the travel gods. You have waited at baggage claim and you are now the last woman standing with no bag. When the travel gods do conspire against you, it is time to swing into action to reunite with your bag.

- **Stay calm and polite.** Honey catches more flies than vinegar. Impatience and anger are a waste of energy.

- **Inquire if there is a different place where early arriving or odd-sized bags are held.** You may find it there if this is your lucky day.

- **Find the office of the carrier** to complete the Lost Baggage Form. That photo of your bag is going to come in handy right about now.

IT'S A NEW WORLD OUT THERE

As a tour escort I have found myself in foreign countries during some turbulent times of terrorism and violence. It is very frightening to not speak the local language and perhaps not have access to reliable news. It is a new world we are navigating.

- **Carry your passport on you.** You do not know if or when you could be separated from your hotel or companions. There is always a danger of becoming ill or being injured. You want first responders to know your identity and where you are from, whether the situation is a natural or manmade disaster. You need your documentation.

- **Register with the U.S. State Department** when traveling abroad. The Smart Traveler Enrollment Program (STEP) is the service that allows you to register your presence in a foreign country. The site is step.state.gov/step/. It is an easy process and will give you and your friends and family at home, some peace of mind.

- **Have your embassy address and phone number in your possession.** They are your first point of contact for any major problem.

- **Have a fully charged cell phone.**

- **Carry a local map.** You need to know where you are and how to move efficiently.

- **Know the local emergency phone number.**

- **Record your emergency contacts and passport information in your phone.**

- **Understand the coverage of your travel insurance.** What aspects of a terror attack does it cover?

- **Have a plan in place to contact home and your travel companions.**

- **Try to have access to a reliable source of international news.** This could be on your phone or Internet.

- **Get a phone number** of where to call for status reports.

- **Record the claim number.**

- **Ask what compensation you are entitled to receive.** It could include an amenity kit with a toothbrush and hygiene products or a voucher for missing items.

- **Hope for the best.** In most cases, your bag will be delivered to you in short order. Luggage is most often not lost permanently, just delayed. The airline should deliver it at no cost to you, but don't go to war over who pays and how you are going to get it.

- Did you buy travel insurance? Most policies cover lost luggage. **Call the insurance carrier's help line** for assistance.

- **Keep receipts for any items you need to purchase.** You may or may not be compensated but only for essentials such as a nightgown or bathing suit. You do not get a whole new Parisian wardrobe.

- **Do not let lost luggage stop you.** What if you go to the captain's cocktail party in your travel clothes? It will give you something to talk about. Slap on a nametag that says, "my luggage is lost" and boldly march forward.

LOSING YOUR PASSPORT

Losing your passport is far worse than losing your way. Where do you begin? Buckle up. You have an expensive and time-consuming "ride" ahead.

- First, try to find it. Retrace your actions, search belongings, and make phone calls to any place that it could have been left. Ask a friend to help. Sometimes a new set of eyes will see what you don't.

- Call the local U.S. Embassy or Consulate. Those numbers should be loaded into your phone or written down. You must go there at your own expense during regular business hours. If it is a weekend or holiday, you have to wait.

- To replace your passport, you will need a completed renewal application and two passport photos, just as if you did when you obtained the original. Additionally, you have to pay for the new document. Make sure you have those funds in cash. They usually do not take credit cards. Having a duplicate copy will expedite getting the new one, but it does not replace it.

- Call your airline if replacing the passport inhibits your ability to take your next flight. Losing your passport does not exempt you from change fees.

CHAPTER 16

All Good Things
Must End

Oh, HOW IT PAINS ME TO TELL YOU THIS, BUT at some point the party is over, and all your sweet anticipation works in reverse: Now the sweetness lies in the memories. The transition from your trip back to reality is tough.

Anticipate the adjustment associated with your return. Set yourself up for success. **Your return is gentler if you can manage some down time before returning to daily life.** This is especially true when you have traveled a long distance or for a long time. Sort the mail, return messages, do the laundry. Most of all, cut yourself some slack.

Treat yourself. A massage or spa treatment is a nice way to prolong the relaxation or recover from the rigors of travel. Keep your calendar clear or light the first few days at home. Manage your jet lag the same way you did at the front of the trip, using a sleep aid if needed. Be careful about driving, operating equipment, and activities requiring balance or coordination until you have had proper sleep and readjusted to your time zone.

Take time to relive your adventures by **going through your photos or working on your scrapbook. Reread your journal** if you kept one. If not, **write about your experiences.** Even if no one ever reads what you wrote, it may help you reflect on your trip. What stands out, and what thoughts and feelings does this evoke?

Refill your toiletry bag. Did you use up all your toothpaste?

Make additions and deletions to your future packing list. What did you learn about your travel style and packing?

Come home to a warm, clean house, and fresh sheets. Do you have a neighbor or friend who can replenish your refrigerator with some basics? How about turning on the heat or AC for you? Stopping at the grocery store on the way home from the airport is a nuisance, but it's also no fun to wake up the next day in a house with no coffee.

Have a meal ready for your return. No matter what time you get home, at some point you're going to need that first meal. Have the ingredients on hand. Better yet, repeat the dinner you ate the night before you left on your trip, because you made extra and popped it in the freezer.

Arrange to have fresh flowers delivered, or pick a bouquet from your garden.

Assess what you learned on this trip that applies to the next. **You can never start planning too early!**

WHERE ARE YOU GOING?

What's keeping you home?

Nobody is guaranteed the gift of another day. If you don't seize the chance to travel now, when will you? Each of us could fill a book with stories about those whose lives have suddenly been altered before they had a chance to fulfill their dreams. Personal circumstances can change and so does the world order. I am grateful for the chances I've had to see places before they were struck by natural or geopolitical disaster, or pandemic.

Investing in travel isn't frivolous. Granted, you must be responsible with your finances. Just don't neglect your "bucket list" or the chance to travel with a loved one. Money is important but so is the quality of your life.

As long as you are breathing, give yourself experiences to take your breath away.

You are ready to take on the world with facts at your fingertips and the tools to make it easy.

Ladies, take heed and take heart. As Thoreau advised, "Go confidently in the direction of your dreams. Live the life you have imagined."

Resource Directory

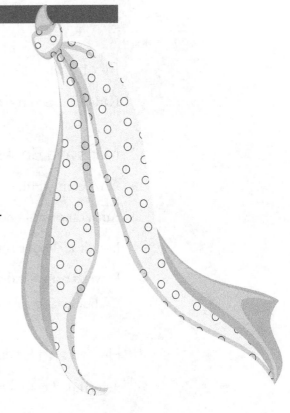

Clothing

Chicos.com – packable clothing in color coordinated families

Coolibar.com – sunblocking clothing and accessories

Magellans.com –especially good for gear and clothing

REI.com – travel and outdoor centered supplies and clothing

Scottevest.com/ygg – travel coats and vests with pockets – Use COUPON CODE YGG for a discount

Talbots.com – clothing that is easy to color coordinate for travel

Travelsmith.com – travel clothing and gear

Wintersilks.com – silk long underwear

Culture and Holidays

Journeywoman.com – excellent resource for what to wear and cultural mores

Timeanddate.com/holidays/ – holidays observed around the world

Electrical

Radioshack.com – adapters and converters

Maps and Books

AAA.com – guidebooks and maps

Amazon.com – books of all types delivered to your door

Longitudebooks.com – lists of travel books fiction and nonfiction

Powells.com – independent bookstore with miles of new and used books and maps

Health and Beauty

Aspirinpod.com – holds two aspirin for travel

Minimus.biz – head to toe products in travel sizes

Money

Oanda.com/currency/travel-exchange-rates – create your own currency conversion chart

Travelex.com – brick and mortar exchanges and online currency ordering service

XE.com – easy online conversion resource

Travel Supplies

Chicobag.com – soft shopping bags

EagleCreek.com – luggage and packing systems

Easytravelerinc.com – system for transferring liquids to travel size
   containers

Scentsy.com – fragrant travel products

TheWineCheck.com – a checked bag to carry a case of wine on
   the plane

To-GoWare.com – bamboo utensils and collapsible bowls

Poopourri.com – guarantees you'll leave the bathroom stink free

Yankeecandle.com – travel candles and products in a variety of
   colors and scents

Passports, Visas and Travel Advisories

Travel.state.gov – instructions for getting or renewing a passport,
   enrollment in STEP and, travel advisories and warnings

Visacentral.com – visa services

Sights and Tickets

Accademia Gallery
   Michelangelo's **David** statue
   Florence, Italy
   B-ticket.com/b-ticket/uffizi/default.aspx

Eiffel Tower
   Paris, France
   toureiffel.paris/en.html

Santa Maria della Gracia

>Milan, Italy

>DaVinci's **Last Supper**

>Vivaticket.it/index.php?nvpg[evento]&id_show=26482

Uffizi Museum

>Florence, Italy

>Botticelli's **Birth of Venus** and more

>B-ticket.com/b-ticket/uffizi/default.aspx

Vatican Museum and Sistine Chapel

>Rome, Italy

>Mv.vatican.va/3_EN/pages/MV_Home.html

9/11 Memorial Museum

>New York City, New York

>911memorial.org/visit

>NOTE: Visits to the memorial are free and open. The museum has an entrance fee. Tickets should be purchased in advance due to limited space and high demand.

Travel/Tour Arrangements and Information

LondonWalks.com – highly rated walking tours of London

Paris-Walks.com – excellent walking tours with superb guides in Paris

Tripadvisor.com – user supplied independent reviews

Weather Forecasts

accuweather.com

theweathernetwork.com

weather.com

wunderground.com

Listings are alphabetical and known to be correct at the time of publication but are subject to change.

About the Author

In MARCIA LYNN MILLER'S FAR-FLUNG ADVENTURES SHE HAS COL-
lected passport stamps from 70 countries while gathering a vast
amount of travel knowledge. Coping with medical emergencies,
lost passports, cancelled flights, and terror threats, while adjusting
to the cultural vagaries of the world, are all in her day's work.

With a degree in economics from the University of Puget
Sound, she finally found career happiness when she pursued
her passion for travel. That has resulted in her being sought out
by women travelers, media, and organizations for consultations,
advice, and speaking engagements on travel-centric topics.

Marcia makes her homes in Portland, Oregon, and on a vineyard property in Zillah, Washington with her husband of 45 years,
and their dog.

Notes

Notes

Notes